# Refinishing Old Furniture

George Wagoner

### TAB Books
#### Division of McGraw-Hill, Inc.
New York  San Francisco  Washington, D.C.  Auckland  Bogotá
Caracas  Lisbon  London  Madrid  Mexico City  Milan
Montreal  New Delhi  San Juan  Singapore
Sydney  Tokyo  Toronto

© 1991 by **George Wagoner**.
Published by TAB Books.
TAB Books is a division of McGraw-Hill, Inc.

Printed in the United States of America. All rights reserved. The publisher takes no responsibility for the use of any of the materials or methods described in this book, nor for the products thereof.

pbk     11  12  13  14  15  16  17  18  19  DOH/DOH  9  9  8  7  6  5  4
hc       4   5   6   7   8   9  10  11  13  DOH/DOH  9  9  8  7  6  5  4

**Library of Congress Cataloging-in-Publication Data**
Wagoner, George.
    Refinishing old furniture / by George Wagoner.
       p.    cm.
    Includes bibliographical references and index.
    ISBN 0-8306-7496-9    ISBN 0-8306-3496-7 (pbk.)
    1. Furniture finishing.  I. Title.
TT199.4.W34   1990
684.1'0443—dc20                             90-43542
                                                    CIP

Acquisitions Editor: Kimberly Tabor
Book Editor: Kathleen E. Beiswenger
Director of Production: Katherine G. Brown
Book Design: Jaclyn J. Boone            TAB1
Cover Design: Lori E. Schlosser       3496

# Contents

**Introduction** — vii

**Before You Begin** — ix
Work area  *ix*
Fire  *x*
Ventilation  *x*
Workbench  *x*
Cabinets  *xi*
Finishing tools  *xi*
Woodworking tools  *xi*
Gloves  *xii*
Eye protection  *xii*
Summary  *xiii*

**1 Choosing the Right Finish** — 1
Finding your first project  *1*
Selecting the right finish  *1*
On-the-surface finishes  *2*
In-the-wood finishes  *9*
Nontoxic finishes  *12*
Basic finishing steps  *14*

**2 Removing Old Finishes** — 16
Using the right paint remover  *16*
Dip tanks  *20*
Tests for finish  *21*
Safety  *21*
Remover application  *22*
Removing milk paint  *26*

**3  Gluing and Clamping**     **27**
    Selecting a glue  *27*
    Gluing and clamping  *30*
    Repairing damaged wood  *33*

**4  Filling Dents and Holes**     **36**
    Applying putty  *36*
    Putty used on bare wood  *38*
    Putty used on finishes  *39*

**5  Sanding**     **41**
    Sanding antiques  *41*
    Sandpaper selection  *42*
    Proper sanding techniques  *45*
    Sanding safety  *47*
    Sanding tools and machines  *47*

**6  Bleaching**     **51**
    Preparing to bleach  *51*
    Choosing the proper bleach  *52*
    Removing red stains  *56*
    Miscellaneous bleaches  *57*

**7  Staining**     **58**
    To stain or not to stain  *58*
    When to use stains  *59*
    Aniline stains  *59*
    Oil stains  *60*
    Oil stain application  *62*
    Woods and stains  *66*
    Glazing  *67*
    Antiquing  *69*

**8  Pore Filling**     **73**
    Paste pore filler application  *73*

**9  Applying Finishes**     **77**
    Sealers  *77*
    Varnish finish application  *79*
    Varnish finish application without a sealer  *79*
    Urethane finishes  *83*
    Preventing and correcting runs  *84*
    Milk paint finish  *85*
    Shellac finish  *86*

French polish finish  *87*
Linseed oil finish  *89*
Tung oil finish  *90*
Penetrating oil finish  *90*
Gilding  *92*
Gold leaf  *92*

## 10  Lacquer Finishing — 94

Lacquer finishing equipment  *94*
Spray guns  *95*
Spraying techniques  *99*
Safety  *104*
Lacquer finish  *104*
Lacquer finish applications  *104*
Types of lacquers  *108*
Distressing  *109*
Finish problems  *111*

## 11  Finishing Unfinished Furniture — 115

Choosing the finish  *118*
Cabinet preparation  *119*
Applying the finish  *125*

## 12  Antique Care and Identification — 129

Restoration  *129*
Cleaning museum-quality furniture  *130*
Identifying antiques  *134*

## 13  Hand-Rubbed Finishes — 137

Finishes and rubbing  *137*
Sanding finishes prior to rubbing  *139*
Flat finish using steel wool  *140*
Semigloss finish using steel wool  *141*
Semigloss finish using pumice stone  *142*
Gloss finish hand-rubbed with rottenstone  *144*
Electric buffer for a high-gloss finish  *146*
Rubbing legs and turnings  *147*

## 14  Polishing — 148

Wiping out advertisements and myths  *148*
Oil polishes  *149*
Wax polishes  *150*
Cream cleaning polishes  *151*
Silicone polishes  *151*
Painted surfaces  *152*

## 15 Touching Up     153
   Simple repairs you can make   *153*
   Burning-in to repair deep dents and scratches   *155*
   Water damage   *160*

## 16 Routine Care of Furniture     161
   Gloss finishes   *161*
   Satin or semigloss   *161*
   Oil finishes   *161*
   Cane furniture   *161*
   Leather care   *162*
   Marble care   *162*
   Polyester wet-look finishes   *163*
   Vinyl care   *163*
   Do's and don'ts for furniture care   *164*

## Appendix     166

## Glossary     168

## Bibliography     172

## Index     175

# Introduction

Refinishing old furniture and antiques has become a popular activity. To some it is a chance to work with their hands or to briefly escape from housework, children, or an office routine. Whatever the reason, refinishing offers an opportunity to make old furniture look like new again. Many older pieces have better wood and construction than the expensive new cabinets that are being manufactured today.

I have taught furniture and antique refinishing classes for 20 years. The information and techniques described in *Refinishing Old Furniture* come from class lecture notes, problems that my students and I have encountered and solved, working with apprentices, and dealing with commercial furniture refinishing.

The purpose of this book is to help the beginner, who knows nothing about finishing, choose the proper techniques to make simple repairs and refinish a project using one of the many finishes and methods outlined in the text. The book is aimed at the beginner, either in a classroom or a do-it-yourselfer at home. The book can also be used in finishing shops to aid a finisher who needs help in a special area. Methods of refinishing antiques are woven through each chapter dealing with refinishing. Chapter 12 is devoted to the care and cleaning of museum-quality furniture, a subject seldom found in refinishing books.

Chapter 11, Finishing Unfinished Furniture, gives photographed step-by-step instruction on how to finish unfinished or "nude" pieces. The chapters on Polishing, Touching Up, and Routine Care of Furniture makes the book valuable to any homemaker.

There are many ways to refinish a piece of furniture. Ask three finishers how to refinish the same chair or table and you will probably hear three different ways, and each would work. If you were able to work with these three finishers, I would tell you to learn all three ways, then choose the methods that are easiest for you, as this book attempts to do.

The finishing materials and application methods outlined in the book range from some of the oldest finishes known to modern up-to-date finishing materials and methods. The finishing steps are presented with easy-to-follow, photographed, step-by-step instructions. The tools needed to refinish are simple and inexpensive. Finishes and finishing materials are easy to find at your local paint, hardware, or building supply store. Hard-to-find supplies can be ordered through the mail from the finishing supply companies listed in the Appendix. Now, go ahead and enjoy yourself. Refinish something.

# Before you begin

Before you begin, you will need a work area where you can remove finishes from your projects, sand the wood, and apply the finishes. Removing finishes is messy, and remover fumes are not healthy to breathe. Sanding creates dust that floats in the air and covers a room. Finishes can give off fumes and need a ventilated, well-lighted, clean, and warm place to be applied and dried.

Garages are good to work in when it is warm, but winter is too cold. A basement, if you have one, can be used in the winter if it is ventilated and warm. A laundry room or spare room could also be used, as could a patio or porch. You can work outside in the summer, but not directly in the sun. Wind and sun quickly dry out paint remover. The sun will blister wet finishes, wind will blow dust that will speckle newly applied finishes, and bugs will just love to crawl on a wet finish.

Your work area should be warm. Glue and finishes need a temperature of 70 degrees or more to dry properly.

Lighting is important, especially when staining and applying finishes. Lights above your work area and, if you can manage, side lighting is helpful. Daylight fluorescent bulbs work well. Good ventilation is a must for your workplace.

## WORK AREA

The fumes from paint removers, solvents, finishes, and sanding dust must be vented or blown outside away from you. When working inside a garage, basement, or room, open an outside door and whatever windows are available. Place a fan in an outside door and another in a window to help move the air out of the room.

To protect the floor from remover spills and finish drips, put a plastic drop cloth under the project. You can also use sheets of cardboard or newspaper to absorb spills. You might be able to find large cardboard boxes at your local furniture store.

Keep your work area clean and organized. When I am working in my garage and applying finishes, I lightly spray the floor with water to hold down dust, and I vacuum the tops of overhead fluorescent light fixtures. It is not a good practice to sand in the same area where finishes will be applied, but if there is no choice, clean the area before applying a finish.

## FIRE

When using finishing materials you must exercise caution. Finishes, finishing solvents, and paint remover liquids are flammable. Keep these materials away from cigarettes, flames, and sparks. As a precaution, keep an approved fire extinguisher close by your work area.

- If there is a gas water heater where you are working, turn off the pilot light before spraying finishes.
- Keep electric heaters away from remover and finishing liquids. If these materials are splashed onto an electric heater, they will burn.
- Store finishes and solvents in an outside cabinet in a garage or shed.
- Soak rags that are used to apply in-the-wood finishes, linseed or tung oil, and penetrating resin sealers in water before disposing of them in a covered metal container. These oily rags will burn by spontaneous combustion if not properly discarded.

## VENTILATION

The fumes from finishing and removing materials are unhealthy to breathe. Always work in an area that is well ventilated. If there is no cross draft, put a fan in an open window or door to circulate air and blow away fumes and dust from spraying or sanding.

Wear a dust mask when sanding or spraying. It is inexpensive and does keep sanding dust and spray particles out of your lungs. If you are working in a confined area and will be exposed to harmful fumes, wear a respirator with charcoal filters for protection.

## WORKBENCH

You will need a sturdy low table or bench in your work area where your project can be placed for repairing or refinishing. The table should be a comfortable height to prevent straining your back by stretching up or bending down. If you do not have a worktable, you can make your own.

To make a simple worktable, place plywood or a hollow core door over two wooden sawhorses. The sawhorses can be adjusted to whatever height is comfortable by sawing off the legs to the desired height. Inexpensive sawhorse brackets are sold at hardware stores. Use 2 × 4s for the cross members and legs. Cut each leg the same length before inserting into the brackets. Make the height of the table about 30 inches. Lay a low pile carpet over the top, wrap it around the plywood and lightly tack it to the underside. Do not put the nails through the top. The nailheads would scratch your furniture.

Finishing shops use turntables, a round table with a lazy Susan-type top that turns in a circle. The project is placed on top of the table and rotated as needed. Turntables are excellent to use when spraying chairs or small pieces.

## CABINETS

Cabinets are handy to store finishing materials and tools. A lock on the cabinet will keep children away.

## FINISHING TOOLS

If the joints on your furniture are tight, and do not require gluing, few tools will be needed. You do not need a whole garage-full of tools to refinish furniture.

To remove a finish, you will need a plastic spatula or wide metal putty knife to push loosened finish off level surfaces.

To apply paint remover you will need steel wool, a coffee can, rags, and an old paintbrush.

To sand, you will need a sandpaper block and sandpaper.

To apply stain, you will need a soft cotton cloth.

To brush on finishes, you will need a 2-inch bristle brush, a coffee can, an old nylon stocking to strain the finish through, and a tack rag to clean the surface prior to applying the finish.

To rub the final coat of finish, you will need steel wool, cream polish, and cotton cloths.

To apply a penetrating resin finish, you will only need cotton cloths to apply the oil to the surface and then to wipe it dry.

Detailed lists of tools and supplies required to complete each step in the finishing process are listed in the appropriate chapters.

## WOODWORKING TOOLS

Woodworking tools are needed to repair furniture with loose joints or broken parts. The basic hand tools that could be used to repair damaged furniture include a lightweight 13-ounce claw hammer with small finishing nails and brads; an assortment of screwdrivers, slotted and Phillips cross-tips; a sharp knife and a retractable utility knife with replaceable blades.

Measuring tools include a tape measure, and a try square with a removable blade to make 90-degree and 45-degree angles for cutting. The try square measuring blade can be removed and used as a guide to cut small wood pieces and veneer.

A four-in-hand wood file is recommended, with both fine and coarse teeth. It is flat on one side and curved on the other to cut flat or curved surfaces.

Wood chisels are used to cut and shape wood. Blade sizes should include $1/4$, $1/2$, and 1 inch.

Also include saws—a crosscut saw to cut large wood pieces and a small, fine-tooth backsaw about 10 inches long with 16 teeth per inch for cutting small wood pieces of veneer. The backsaw has a rectangular blade stiffened by a metal bar across the top. A hypodermic-like glue injector is used to force glue into joints and under veneers.

Other tools that are useful are pliers, diagonal pliers, nail punch, hacksaw, wood clamps, adjustable wrench, vise, rubber mallet, drill and bits, and a jack plane.

For centuries, furniture was made with simple hand tools. The old craftsmen made fine furniture without the use of electric power tools, often surpassing modern machine-manufactured furniture. Although not essential, power tools can make repairing furniture much easier, however.

A well-equipped shop should have an electric drill with a 3/8-inch chuck and an assortment of drill bits. Attach a screwdriver bit to the drill, and it can be used as a power screwdriver. Consider a portable, cordless, battery-powered drill. A hand-held skill saw to cut plywood and boards, a saber saw to cut small curved parts, and an electric buffer to buff finishes to a high gloss are other options for your shop.

## GLOVES

Many years ago when I began my finishing apprenticeship, my first job was to strip finishes off furniture using paint remover, a job given to beginning apprentices. After a few days of using paint remover and solvents, the skin on my hands dried out, cracked, and peeled off. No one in the shop used rubber gloves. Eventually, I moved on to staining, applying stains to wood. This promotion was several rungs up the ladder from finish removing. Now my hands were in stains all day. My hands changed from dried out and peeling to dried out, peeling, and covered with dark stain.

With age comes wisdom. Now I can spend a day working in paint remover or stains, and my hands are clean and soft. The answer, of course, is wearing chemical-resistant rubber gloves or applying hand-protect cream when working with solvents.

To protect your hands when staining or applying finishes, wear the inexpensive surgical gloves found in paint stores and drugstores. If your hands do become stained, wash the dishes—the detergent might clean them. If that does not work, try soaking your hands in laundry bleach. Be careful not to overdo soaking in bleach as it can also dry out your skin.

There are chemical-resistant creams that protect skin from paint removers, finishes, and stains. Rub the cream on your hands before working, then wash off with soap and warm water when the job is finished. These creams also are called hand-protect cream or liquid glove. Look for them in your paint or hardware store.

## EYE PROTECTION

Buying and wearing an inexpensive pair of plastic safety glasses is important. It can keep splashed paint remover, finishing solvents, sanding dust, and bits and pieces of wood thrown off by power tools out of your eyes.

If paint remover or other finishing liquids splash into your eyes, immediately stop working and go to a sink and flood your eyes with water. Use a clean hand as a cup under the faucet and flow water into your eyes. A well-equipped shop should have an eye wash bottle in the first aid kit.

Plastic lenses on glasses and contact lenses can be pitted by splashes from removing and finishing solvents.

## SUMMARY

Do not let the do's and don'ts deter your enthusiasm for finishing. With a little knowledge and care, you will avoid these problems and have an enjoyable time refinishing your furniture.

# Chapter 1

# Choosing the right finish

*E*ach step in the finishing process can be a rewarding experience for you. You can identify the wood, see the grain and its pattern, watch the wood turn a beautiful color when it is stained, and apply the finish and rub it. Then, when it is finished, you can stand back and say, "That looks great."

## FINDING YOUR FIRST PROJECT

Your first decision when you begin refinishing is choosing your first project. If there is nothing at home to refinish, try the antique shops. They are best but are usually too expensive. Garage sales can be a good source, sometimes a great one. Relatives' attics, thrift shops, auctions, and the city dump are all places to explore.

Choose a small project, for it is easy to become discouraged if you overextend yourself. Try something that is not too difficult—a small end table or simple chair. Taking on a large dining room table with six chairs could become a disaster, leaving you with a real dislike for finishing.

Do not buy a chair or table just because it is inexpensive. Avoid antiques that have too many parts missing or are badly split and broken, unless you are a craftsman who has the tools to make parts. Spend a little more money and buy a piece that has all its parts and, if possible, tight joints. The finish is not important; you are going to put on a new one.

Finishing a piece of furniture should not only serve a functional purpose, that is, getting more use out of it, but should also be enjoyable. To find a walnut, cherry, or other fine wood under several coats of paint is rewarding and exciting.

## SELECTING THE RIGHT FINISH

Almost every man-made object has some kind of finish on it: houses, appliances, automobiles, and furniture. You are surrounded by furniture everywhere you go. You sleep, eat, sit, and work with it. You might not always realize how important furniture is, but you would be lost without its use.

Once you decide to refinish a piece of furniture, you must also decide which finish to use. There are many different kinds available. If you are not familiar with the finishes, it can be difficult to know which ones will work with your project. Pay special attention to the descriptions of finishes in this chapter. Both old and new are described along with their best points and problems. Then choose the coating best-suited for the project and its use.

## Finish qualities

Try to find a finish that has these qualities. Look for:

1. A permanent coating that does not rub off with wear or wash off with solvents.
2. A coating that protects wood from sun and moisture:
   - Water resistant—does not crack, peel, or turn white when exposed to water;
   - Ultraviolet ray resistant—does not rapidly fade or crack when exposed to the sun.
3. A coating that protects the wood from the hazards of daily use and resists:
   - Acids from food,
   - Moisture from spilled water,
   - Alcohol from spilled drinks,
   - Resists denting and scratching.
4. A good-looking finish.
5. An easy-to-apply finish that flows out smoothly and has a depth of appearance.

## Properties of a finish

A finish consists of:

1. *Pigment*—color.
2. *Vehicle* or *binder*—the liquid that binds the pigment particles together and gives strength; it is the tough paint film.
3. *Thinner* or *solvent*—evaporates after application; does not form a film; flows out the materials; and holds the color and paint film in suspension.

Finishes are divided into two groups: on-the-surface finishes and in-the-wood finishes.

## ON-THE-SURFACE FINISHES

The first group of finishes are the on-the-surface finishes. Here the finish produces a tough film on the surface of the wood, giving a smooth surface with an appearance of depth. This is a finish you can see and see through, or a finish that has color added to it, or an opaque finish. Examples of on-the-surface finishes are shellac, varnish, urethane, lacquer, and paints. These products are pictured in FIG. 1-1. Detailed finishing steps are described in Chapter 9, *Applying Finishes*.

**1-1** On-the-surface finishes.

## Milk paint

Many early American pieces were finished with colored milk paint. Red, black, and green colors were often used. The paint was made with skim milk or buttermilk and colored with local materials. Lamp black (soot from the chimneys of oil lamps), berry juice, burnt clay, and dry colors were used. This paint was considered desirable and was painted on houses and furniture.

Although no longer used, milk paint is mentioned because it is difficult to remove from wood and will need special attention (see Chapter 2, "*Removing Old Finishes*"). Casein paints are the modern equivalent of milk paint.

## Shellac

Shellac is the oldest on-the-surface finish. It has been known since 1500 B.C. and was used until around 1860. It was occasionally used up to 1930.

Shellac is imported from India where it is made by a small insect, the lac bug (Tachardia lalla). The lac bug feeds on resins of the acacia tree, excreting the lac through its pores, encasing itself and the twigs where it is feeding. The twigs are removed and the shellac is cleaned off the twigs and heated. The lac is then stretched into large sheets. When cool, it is broken into small pieces called *shellac crystals*. These crystals are dissolved in denatured alcohol. Because raw shellac is orange or amber in color, it is called *orange shellac*, which is not an unpleasant color when brushed on wood. Paint manufacturers remove this color by bleaching; it is then called *white shellac*.

**4** *Choosing the right finish*

**1-2** This ladder-back chair was finished with three coats of shellac.

The early finishers applied shellac with a brush or by French polishing. To French polish, the finisher rubs shellac onto the wood with a soft pad soaked with thinned shellac and lubricated with oil. The finisher slowly builds up a fine durable finish by rubbing shellac onto the piece, rubbing across the surface in a circular pattern. Although seldom used today, French polishing was highly regarded by early day furniture finishers.

Shellac is an excellent sealer. It seals knots and stops pitch and sap from seeping into top coats. It prevents stains from bleeding out of wood into top coats, especially red aniline stains. It has been used as a sealer under varnish, lacquer, and paint. Shellac is a good-looking, durable finish when used alone. The chair in FIG. 1-2 was finished with shellac.

Shellac's problems outweigh its good points and restrict its use now that newer finishes are available. These problems are:

1. Shellac is hygroscopic. It absorbs moisture from the air and can turn white when it comes in contact with water.
2. Shellac dissolves in alcohol. If an alcoholic drink spills on the surface, it softens and melts the finish.

Because of these problems, shellac is best used as a sealer with a more durable finish applied over it.

## Varnish

Varnish was used from about 1850 until 1927. The early varnishes were made by boiling natural oils and resins.

Varnish is a tough, durable finish that is water and alcohol resistant. It is a hard finish that is resistant to abrasions. It rubs well and looks excellent on fine furniture, as the old rocker in FIG. 1-3 shows. Varnish is made to be rubbed.

A few of varnish's problems are:

1. Varnish is slow drying and must be brushed on.
2. Each coat takes two or more warm days to dry.
3. Because varnish dries slowly, any dust that lands on the wet surface becomes imbedded in the finish, requiring rubbing as a final finishing step.

The old varnish finishing rooms had wood floors that were oiled to hold down dust. Doors and windows were sealed to keep out dust.

There are two types of varnishes. The first dries hard throughout the coating and is made to be used on furniture. It might be labeled *interior*, *furniture*, or *rubbing varnish*.

The second, *spar varnish*, should not be used on furniture. Spar varnish is not recommended for furniture because it is soft and can soften in warm weather. Spar varnish is made to be used on exterior surfaces where it can expand and contract with changing temperatures without cracking.

**1-3** This rocker was finished with three coats of varnish.

Varnish is made by boiling natural oils and resins from trees. It is combined, under heat and pressure, with dryers to speed the drying process. *Spirit varnish* (synthetic) *film* dries when the thinner evaporates, as does lacquer, shellac, and urethane.

Several types of varnish are:

- *Oleoresinous varnish*—contains drying oils and resin. Soft resin is left to air-dry. Air finishes the drying process. Linseed and tung oil also dry in this way.
- *Alkyd resin varnish*—quick-drying synthetic varnish made from chemicals and oils. Alkyds containing tung oils are best. Used for coating interior furniture and wood work.
- *Rosin/ester gum alkyd varnish*—dries to a hard film, has excellent wearing qualities, and is good for gym floors.
- *Phenolic-resin varnish*—for outside use only. This weather-resistant finish stays soft and flexible. Not a good choice for interior furniture, but excellent when used on exterior wood that is exposed to sun and weather. Contains phenolic resin, tung oil, and ultraviolet absorbers.
- *Urethane resin*—(with tung oil) a hard interior finish for bar tops, kitchen cabinets, and family room furniture.

## Urethanes

Urethanes are varnish-like finishes that are made from chemicals rather than natural oils and resins. By using chemicals, the chemist can make these finishes tougher and dry faster than varnish. Other urethane-type finishes are *varathane* and *polyurethane*.

Urethanes are hard, durable coatings highly resistant to abrasions, scratching, water, chemicals, grease, solvents, food stains, alcohol, and oils. These finishes are best used on high-wear surfaces. They are excellent for family room furniture, kitchen cabinets, tabletops, bar tops, and children's furniture, FIG. 1-4.

**1-4** This bentwood chair was finished with two coats of urethane.

Some problems with urethanes are:

1. Not all urethanes are resistant to ultraviolet radiation.
2. Urethanes have a tough surface that is hard to rub.
3. Some urethanes cannot be applied over shellac, lacquer, varnish, or stains that contain a stearate dryer. Read and follow the label instructions.

Buy oil-soluble urethane, that is, one that is thinned with paint thinner. Avoid urethanes that are hardened with a catalyst or thinned with water.

## Enamel

Early enamels were made by mixing varnish and pigment. The result was a colored paint that dried to a smooth, hard, glossy finish. Modern enamels are made by mixing varnish resins and chemicals with color or by adding colors to the hard urethane finishes. There is also an enamel latex paint that is thinned with water.

Enamels are identified by their hard, smooth, colored surface. They can vary in sheen from high gloss to satin.

## Lacquer

Lacquer is a fast-drying finish that is tough and durable and easy to sand, rub, and repair. Furniture that takes several days to finish with varnish can be finished with lacquer in a few hours. Because lacquer dries rapidly, it must be sprayed, with the exception of slow-drying brushing lacquer. The rocker in FIG. 1-5 was sprayed with lacquer.

Prior to 1924, varnish was the principal finishing material used. When lacquer was introduced after World War I, the use of varnish in factories stopped. Lacquer became and remains the main finish used by furniture manufacturers and finishing shops. Lacquer is available in gloss,

**1-5** This rocker was sprayed with two coats of lacquer sanding sealer, then sprayed with two coats of satin lacquer.

satin, flat, water clear, sanding sealer, and a myriad of colors and special finishes.

Some good points about lacquer:

1. Lacquer is fast drying and does not accumulate dust while it dries.
2. Lacquer has a hard finish and sands well.
3. Lacquer is resistant to water and alcohol.
4. Lacquer is easy to repair.
5. Many varieties of finishes and finishing methods can be used with lacquer.
6. Lacquer can be used safely on food containers and children's furniture.

Some problems with lacquer:

1. Lacquer is not completely water or alcohol proof.
2. Lacquer is for indoor use only.
3. Lacquer is not as tough as varnish or urethane.
4. Lacquer film is thin. Several coats must be applied to build up a thick finish.
5. Lacquer must be sprayed unless a special brushing lacquer is used.

Lacquer is made by melting a nitrocellulose, or buttrate, in alcohol, kentone, or ester solvents. Then resins are added. The resins can be ester gum, maleic, or phenolic resins, or any combination of these or hundreds of special alkyd or resin-modified materials.

- *Nitrocellulose* gives toughness and strength.
- *Plasticizer* gives flexibility and bending.
- *Resins* give adhesion, gloss, and durability.
- *Solvents* dissolve and hold particles in suspension and help the finish to flow out and dry rapidly.

## IN-THE-WOOD FINISHES

The second group of finishes are in-the-wood finishes. These finishes penetrate into the wood, hardening the inner fibers without a noticeable surface film. They are used with casual contemporary furniture. They lack the depth and formal look of the on-the-surface finishes. Examples are linseed oil, tung oil, and penetrating resin sealer. The products are pictured in FIG. 1-6. Detailed finishing steps are described in Chapter 9, *Applying Finishes*.

### Linseed oil

Linseed oil has been used on wood for thousands of years. It was used on wood found in the Egyptian tombs. Linseed oil is extracted from the

**1-6** In-the-wood finishes: linseed oil, tung oil, and penetrating resin sealer.

seeds of the flax plant. This oil protects woods that are exposed to air, sun, and moisture. The oil forms a resinous coating that penetrates into the wood, closes the pores, and prevents destructive agents from entering. It resists alcohol, water, and food acids, and also prevents decay, warping, shrinking, and splitting. There is no thick coating to chip. If there is a dent or scratch to repair, simply sand off the damaged spot and reoil.

Some problems with linseed oil are:

1. Linseed oil is slow to apply.
2. Linseed oil becomes gummy on opened pored wood and carvings if it is not rubbed dry between coats.
3. Linseed oil darkens wood.
4. The rags used to apply linseed oil can burn by spontaneous combustion and must be disposed of in a covered container.

Because a linseed oil finish is not waterproof, it should be varnished over to produce a more durable surface on kitchen and family room tables. Linseed oil produces a dull finish that looks best on hard, fine-grained wood. Good examples are walnut, cherry, teak, and rosewood.

Use boiled linseed oil on furniture. It dries throughout the coating.

Do not use raw linseed oil on furniture, it does not dry hard. This product is made to be used outdoors. It stays pliable and will not crack when exposed to changing exterior temperatures and humidity. Although excellent for outside use, it is too soft to be used on furniture.

### Tung oil (China wood oil)

Tung oil has been used as a finishing material for centuries. This oil is extracted from the nuts of the tung tree, which is native to China. Tung oil produces a hard, clear, in-the-wood finish that is resistant to water, acid, alkali, and mildew.

Tung oil comes in three forms:

1. *Pure tung oil* is oil pressed from tung nuts and filtered.
2. *Tung seed* tung oil is dissolved in thinner with a dryer added.
3. *Polymerized tung oil* has been heat-treated and is the best to use. It dries hard and gives the highest gloss.

The finish can be applied with a brush, rag, or your hands. The oil is rubbed into the wood, then wiped dry. Up to three coats can be applied.

Tung oil is superior to linseed oil; it dries faster, harder, and is twice as moisture resistant. Thin coats dry dull; heavy coats dry glossy but can wrinkle. Tung oil has a short shelf life; once exposed to air it begins to harden in the container, even though the lid is tightly resealed. The rags used to apply the oil can burn by spontaneous combustion and must be disposed in a covered metal container. Tung oil can be varnished over to obtain a more durable surface, especially on kitchen and family room tables. Tung oil is an excellent waterproofing agent and is used in quality varnishes.

## Penetrating resin sealers

Commercially prepared penetrating resin sealer is a modern in-the-wood finish that is probably the easiest finish to use. Penetrating sealers are mixtures of oil and varnish-like resins that penetrate deep into the wood. Once this coating dries, it gives the wood a tough, wearable surface without any noticeable coating film. It actually toughens and hardens the wood. It will not chip or peel and is far superior to linseed oil.

Some other advantages are that penetrating sealers do not gum up, become oily, or darken with age. It is easy to use. Apply it with a brush, rag, or rub on with your hands; let it soak in; then wipe it dry. The chair in FIG. 1-7 was finished with a penetrating resin sealer.

Penetrating sealers are used by home finishers, cabinet shops, and factories producing modern Danish furniture. They are sold in paint and hardware stores.

## Wax finish

Confusion is common regarding wax finishes. When a furniture finisher uses the term "wax finish," he usually means that a penetrating sealer or shellac finish has been applied to the wood and then polished with a paste wax. This is a simple and acceptable finish.

A wax finish also might refer to several coats of hard paste wax applied to bare or stained wood and polished between coats. Very simple except it is not a finish. A finish is a permanent coating that does not rub off with wear or wash off with solvents. Wax alone will come off with wear and solvents.

The use of wax alone as a finish could be justified if a valuable antique was being refinished, and you were unsure of which finish to use. The wax would not harm the antique and could later be washed off with paint thinner.

## 12  *Choosing the right finish*

**1-7** Before and after. The chair has been restored and finished with two coats of penetrating resin sealer.

## NONTOXIC FINISHES

Nontoxic finishes are finishes used on food utensils and children's toys. They should be free of compounds that, if ingested, are not dangerous. Finishes made with dryers containing lead or mercury pose the greatest threat. A child can quickly chew or suck the finish from a wooden toy.

*Nontoxic finishes* **13**

**1-8** After the finish is removed, the wood is lightly sanded.

Toxic compounds on wooden bowls and utensils can leach out of the finish and be ingested with the food. The safety products division of the U.S. Food and Drug Administration states that their main concern is with the presence of lead and mercury in a finishing material. If a finish does not contain lead or other metals, the finish can be considered nontoxic and acceptable for food service and toys.

Finishing materials that meet these criteria are:

1. Clear wood finishing lacquers
2. Water-based or latex varnishes
3. Watco brand oil finish, which is safe to use after it has dried for 30 days. This waiting period is necessary to allow the oil to completely harden.

## BASIC FINISHING STEPS

The following list contains the basic steps for an average finish. This list is not complete nor does it apply to all types of finishes:

1. If necessary, remove the old finish.
2. Reglue loose joints or broken parts.
3. Fill dents with putty.
4. Sand the wood smooth (FIG. 1-8).
5. Apply stain to add color if desired (FIG. 1-9).
6. Apply a sealer coating and sand it.
7. Apply one or more coats of finish.
8. Rub the finish (FIG. 1-10).

1-9  The stain is applied to the sanded wood.

Basic finishing steps 15

**1-10** The finish is applied and hand rubbed.

# Chapter 2

# Removing old finishes

*B*efore you put paint remover on your furniture to take the old finish off, stop and examine the item. The finish might not need to be removed.

On new furniture made after 1930, try to clean the finish. Use a cloth dampened with water and a mild detergent. Next, clean it with 4/0 steel wool that has been dipped in paint thinner and gently rub the finish following the grain of the wood. When the furniture has a gloss finish, forego the use of steel wool because it could dull the shiny surface. Instead, use a cloth and paint thinner.

After the finish is clean, the final step is to polish the finish with a cream cleaning polish. If the finish is varnish, use an oil polish or real lemon oil.

On old furniture made before 1930, do not use water to clean the finish. It might be shellac, and water could turn the finish white or hazy. Instead, use 4/0 steel wool and paint thinner. Clean a gloss finish with a rag dampened with paint thinner, then polish with a cream cleaning polish.

Should the cleaning process restore the finish and make the piece look good, do not take the finish off. Use the piece as is and enjoy it. Finishes that you do not like should be removed. Coatings that are flaking, peeling, disintegrated, or worn away should also be removed (see FIGS. 2-1 and 2-2).

## USING THE RIGHT PAINT REMOVER

*Paint removers* are liquids that are applied to furniture to remove the old finish from its surface. The finish can be lacquer, varnish, sealers, oils, or paints. Removing tools and materials are pictured in FIG. 2-3. Two basic kinds of removers are wax-type removers and wax-free removers.

*Using the right paint remover*   **17**

**2-1**  Remove finishes that are flaking and peeling.

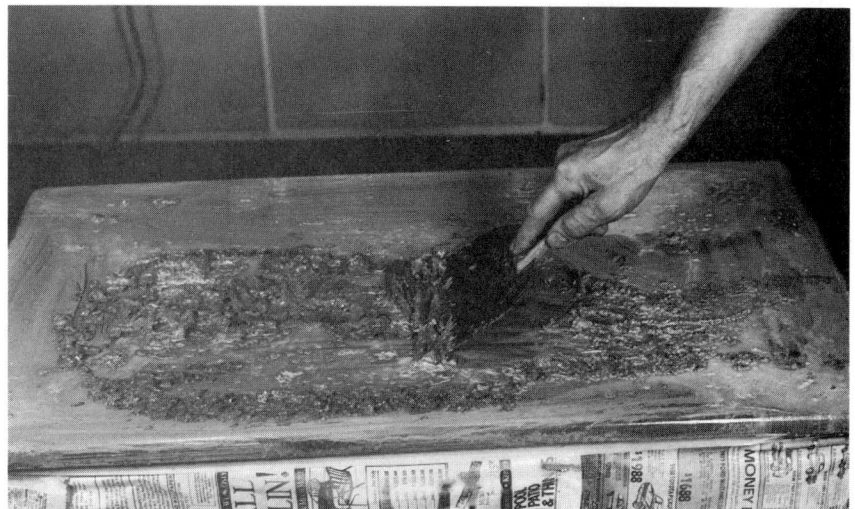

**2-2**  Loosen an old finish with paint remover, then push it off with a wide putty knife.

### Wax-type removers

As the name implies, wax-type removers contain wax. They might be made with mixtures of paraffin wax, benzol, alcohol, lacquer thinner, acetone, or methanol. Wax is added to the remover to form a surface film that slows evaporation of the remover when it is laying on the finish.

It is extremely important that this wax is thoroughly washed off the wood after the finish has been removed. If this wax is not completely removed, the finish that is later applied might not dry.

## 18  Removing old finishes

**2-3** Tools and materials that can be used to remove finishes.

Some good points about wax removers:

- Mild removers
- Do not raise the grain
- Do not darken or lighten wood
- Do not open pores
- Dry immediately

Some bad points about wax removers:

- Evaporate rapidly
- Flammable
- Fumes are bad to breathe
- Work slowly on multiple coats of paint
- Wax left on the wood can later cause a wet finish
- Have a thin consistency

To tell the difference between a remover that contains wax and one that does not, read the label on the can. If it says wash the remover off the wood with lacquer thinner, paint thinner, alcohol, or a solvent, then it has wax in it. If the label tells you to clean the remover off with water, or to just wipe the wood clean with a rag, then it should not contain wax.

A formula for wax-type removers is:

1. Pour 2 gallons of benzol in a can.
2. Melt three bars of paraffin wax.
3. Slowly pour the melted wax into the benzol and stir briskly.

4. Add 2 gallons denatured alcohol. Pour it in slowly and stir it briskly.
5. Lacquer thinner and acetone can also be added.

The following solvents can be used to wash off wax-type removers: lacquer thinner, denatured alcohol, benzol, paint thinner, turpentine, and acetone.

### Wax-free removers

The second type of removers are wax free. These removers might contain methylene chloride and toluene. They might contain flammable solvents. Some are cleaned off the wood with water; others are wiped off with a dry rag.

These removers are usually thick and excellent to use on vertical surfaces where they can cling without running off. Use thin removers on horizontal surfaces where they cannot run off.

Some good points about wax-free removers are:

- They contain no wax.
- Many are not flammable.
- They usually have a thick consistency.

Some bad points about wax-free removers are:

- Water used to clean off water-wash removers is bad for wood because it might loosen veneers, raise the grain, open pores, and loosen glue joints.
- They are slow drying and might take a day or more for the water to dry.
- Methylene chloride used in some of these removers is harmful to breathe.

To avoid the problems that water can cause, use lacquer thinner instead of water to wash off the remover. Lacquer thinner is a mild remover; it will clean the wood and remove any finish missed by the remover. Because lacquer thinner dries rapidly, you can begin working on the wood immediately. When water is used to wash the wood, it is necessary to wait one day for the water to dry.

### Homemade removers to avoid

**Lye** Lye, or caustic soda (toilet bowl cleaner), when mixed and used properly is an inexpensive and effective remover. Use it only on difficult removing projects.

If not properly used, lye can cause considerable damage to wood. It darkens pine, maple, mahogany, cherry, and oak. Lye can also burn wood, etch it, and actually eat it away. Lye can open pores, raise the grain, and burn your skin, eyes, and clothes.

You can lighten wood darkened by lye by bleaching with oxalic acid. Mix 2 ounces of oxalic acid crystals with 1 pint of hot water. Wet the wood with this mixture. It will miraculously lighten the wood (see Chapter 6, *Bleaches*).

To make an effective lye remover, add one 13-ounce can of toilet bowl cleaner (caustic soda) to 1 quart of hot water. Mix them in a pail, but not an aluminum or plastic one because lye produces a poisonous gas when it comes in contact with aluminum.

Remove the finish outside in the sun. Use an old paintbrush to apply the lye solution. Keep the finish wet with remover. When the paint softens and begins peeling, use a wide putty knife to carefully push off the loosened paint. Use a bristle brush to scrub away stubborn paint. When the finish is gone, wash off the piece with water. You can spray it off with a water hose. Wipe the water off and set the piece aside to dry for a day before you begin finishing.

Pour lye into water, not water into lye because it might boil up. Remember, do not use an aluminum pail because toxic fumes will be produced. For problems with water, read the information for water-wash removers in the previous section.

**Ammonia** Ammonia is another effective remover, but like lye, it darkens many woods and the fumes are strong and unpleasant. Use ammonia to remove milk paint. Mix it with trisodium phosphate (T.S.P.) to remove milk paint that commercial removers will not soften. If you can find it, use full-strength ammonia. It is much stronger than household ammonia. You might be able to buy it from a chemical firm.

**Trisodium phosphate** T.S.P. is similar to lye, but milder, and is commonly used as a cleaner. Painters use it to wash and dull painted surfaces prior to painting. Mixed with hot water, T.S.P. is excellent to clean off water-wash removers. Mixed with ammonia, it helps remove milk paint. Because T.S.P. is a mild lye, it can also darken wood, but the darkened wood can be lightened by bleaching with oxalic acid. To use as a cleaner, add 1/2 cup T.S.P. to 1 gallon water. Most hardware and paint stores stock T.S.P.

## DIP TANKS

If you want to save a lot of work, take those pieces with hard-to-remove finishes, especially painted chairs, to a finishing shop that has a dip tank.

Dip tanks can be great or horrible, depending on what remover and methods are used. A piece of furniture is lowered into a tank that is filled with remover and soaked until the finish comes off. It is then pulled out, and the remover and any remaining finish is cleaned from the surface. It sure beats spending hours in the garage up to your elbows in paint remover. All it takes is money.

Sounds easy, and it can be if a mild remover is used in the tank, and the remover is cleaned off the wood with lacquer thinner or similar solvent. The problem is that commercial removers are expensive, especially to fill a large tank, and they are flammable. The fire department puts restrictions on their use. To get around the cost and restrictions, most finishing shops use lye remover. Lye is cheap, effective, not flammable, and is cleaned off with water. Great for the finishing shop, but not for your furniture.

The problem with lye is that it works too well. When a piece of wood comes out of a lye dip tank, the wood, if there is any left, can be etched and eaten away, and its pores puffed and open. Many woods are darkened, veneers peel off, and glue joints loosened. When the piece is out of the tank, it is hosed off with water, further damaging the wood. If it has been blackened by lye, it is lightened with oxalic acid. You are left with little natural color. It can look like an old bone that has been bleaching in the sun for years.

If you decide to use a commercial dip tank for finish removal, be sure there is a mild commercial remover in it, not lye. Even though it costs more, it is best to have the piece hand-stripped with a commercial remover and cleaned off with lacquer thinner (see "Lye Remover").

## TESTS FOR FINISH

If you need to identify the finish on your furniture, one of the following tests might work:

**Lacquer test** On an obscure part of the piece, wet the finish with lacquer thinner and keep it wet for several minutes. If the finish softens or melts, it is lacquer. Most factory-applied on-the-surface finishes are lacquer. Use paint remover to take it off. Lacquer thinner will work, but it is slow.

**Shellac test** Shellac will melt when rubbed with alcohol or lacquer thinner. Shellac was used on furniture made before 1860; it is not used on modern furniture. Use paint remover to remove shellac.

**Varnish test** Once hardened, varnish cannot be softened or removed with a mild solvent. Briskly rubbing the finish with the palm of your hand will heat the finish, and if it is varnish, release its characteristic odor. Paint remover must be used to remove varnish.

**Urethane test** This hard finish is not affected by solvents or rubbing. Paint remover is the only sure way to remove it.

**Oil finishes test** If the wood looks unfinished or oiled with open pores, it might have an in-the-wood finish, such as linseed oil, tung oil, or penetrating resin sealer. Paint remover must be used to remove these finishes.

## SAFETY

Paint removers can burn your skin and eyes. Protect your hands by applying hand protecting cream or wearing rubber gloves. Wear safety goggles to protect your eyes from splashes. Use soap and water to clean remover from your skin. Wash remover from your eyes by flooding them with water. Breathing fumes from removers that contain methylene chloride can cause carbon monoxide to enter the blood, particularly bad for elderly people and people with heart problems.

Removers and thinners are flammable. When using removers and thinners, take the following precautions:

1. Avoid breathing fumes.
2. Have adequate ventilation.
3. Keep flammable removers away from cigarettes, fires, sparks, and electric and gas heaters.
4. Do not take internally.
5. Wash hands after using.

## REMOVER APPLICATION

Remove all drawers, doors, mirrors, and parts that can be easily disassembled (FIG. 2-4). Store hardware in a can for safekeeping. Use masking tape and newspaper to mask off parts that are not being treated. Spread paper or cardboard under the project to catch remover drippings. If you are working outside, work in the shade. Avoid drafts; sun and wind quickly dry out remover. Place the surface being removed in a horizontal position; thin removers will run off vertical surfaces. Wear old clothes, a long sleeve shirt, and rubber gloves.

**2-4** Remove all handles and parts that are easy to disassemble.

Shake the remover can to mix the solvents, unless the instructions on the container say not to. Pour into a can; a coffee can is excellent. With an old paintbrush, apply a heavy, wet, even coat of remover (FIG. 2-5). Brush in one direction, not back and forth. Apply to one area at a time, not the entire piece. After removing the finish on one side, turn the project so another side is in a horizontal position, then remove the finish on that side. Continue until the entire piece is cleaned.

When a surface is covered with remover, do not scrub, brush, or disturb the wet surface. Wax in the remover has formed a surface film that

**2-5** Apply a heavy, wet coat of paint remover.

slows evaporation. If this film is disturbed, the remover will quickly evaporate. To work properly, remover must be applied wet and heavy; dried remover will not work. Allow the remover to lie wet on the finish from 10 to 30 minutes until the finish wrinkles off, or until you are able to rub through to the next layer of paint or bare wood.

Use a wide putty knife to gently push the loose finish off, but you must be careful because a putty knife can easily gouge the wood surface (FIG. 2-6). Use 2/0 or 3/0 steel wool, wet with remover, to scrub off stubborn finish. If necessary, apply a second and third coat of remover.

When the finish is gone, start at the top of the project and wash off the remover. Scrub the wood with 2/0 or 3/0 steel wool that is soaked with lacquer thinner. Clean the wood with the grain. Scrub away all remaining remover, finish, and wax. As you clean, keep in mind that wax is invisible, so the cleaning must be thorough. When the upper surface is clean, wash off the sides, then down the legs, flooding and floating away the wax with lacquer thinner (FIG. 2-7).

Water can be used to clean away water-wash strippers on solid wood but not on veneered wood. Water can soften old glue, and veneers might loosen and peel. To be safe, use lacquer thinner in place of water. Lacquer thinner is a mild remover that will clean off any remaining finish and clean the wood without the problems water could cause.

While the finish is soft and wet with stripper, clean grooves with a short stiff-bristle brush, toothbrush, soft-wire suede brush, or steel wool. The suede brush is excellent to use to clean white paint out of pores. To clean finish out of the grooves of round table and chair legs, use a string with steel wool wrapped around it. Place the string and steel wool in the groove and pull back and forth (FIG. 2-8). Porous end grain that has a light-

## 24 Removing old finishes

**2-6** Push off the loosened finish, being careful not to scratch the wood.

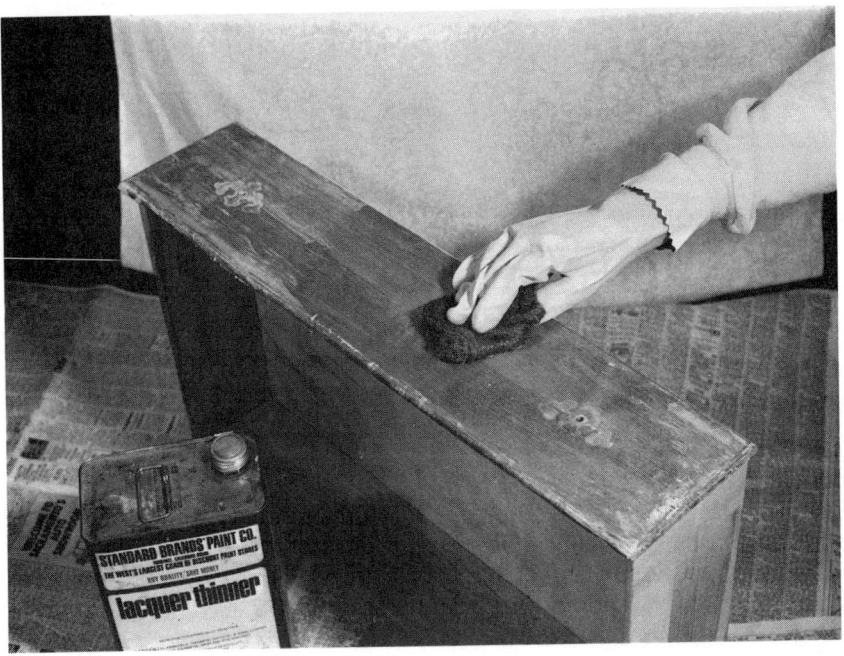

**2-7** Scrub off any remaining remover and old finish with steel wool and lacquer thinner.

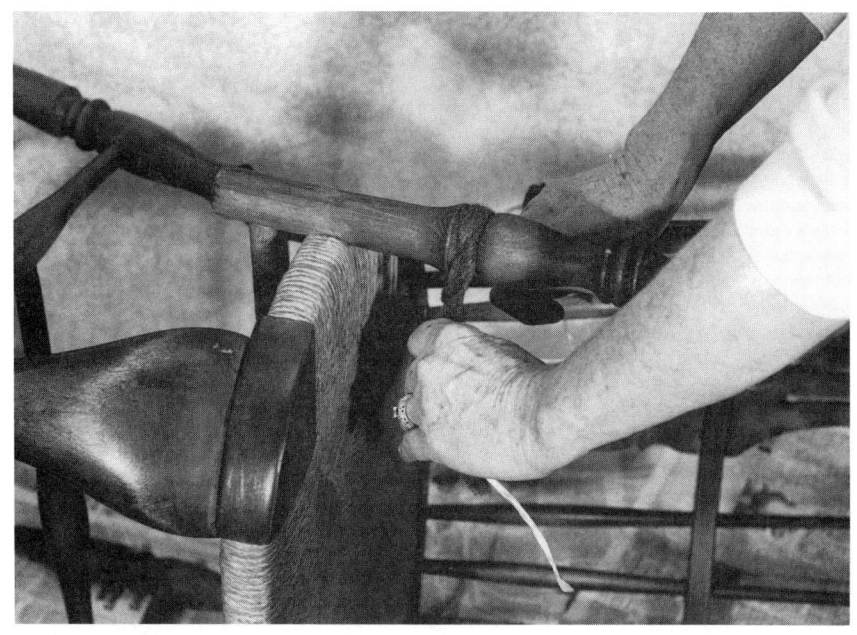

**2-8** Wrap steel wool around string or rope to clean grooves of turnings.

colored finish embedded in it might need to be sanded clean or colored over.

The most important step in the removing process is to thoroughly remove the stripper and all wax from the wood. If wax is left on the wood, a finish applied over it will not dry and leave shiny, sticky wet spots on the finish that are difficult to correct (see finish problems in Chapter 10, *Lacquer Finishing*).

If water is used to clean off the remover residue, mix ½ cup of T.S.P. with 1 gallon of hot water. Wash off any remaining stripper and finish with this mixture, rinse with clean water, and wipe dry.

*Materials:*

Remover

Coffee can

Lacquer thinner

Paintbrush

Dull putty knife

Rags

2/0 or 3/0 steel wool

Scrub brushes (stiff-bristle brush, toothbrush, or soft brass suede brush)

Hand-protecting cream or rubber gloves

*Application*

1. Remove hardware.
2. Place paper under the project.
3. Shake or stir the remover. Pour it into coffee can.
4. Apply a heavy, wet coat of remover.
5. Allow the remover to work. Leave it wet on the surface until the finish softens—about 10-30 minutes.
6. Push off the finish with a dull putty knife.
7. Scrub the surface with 2/0 or 3/0 steel wool soaked with remover.
8. Clean the wood with a rag.
9. Scrub the wood with 2/0 steel wool soaked with lacquer thinner. Flood the wood with the thinner.
10. Do a final cleaning with a rag and lacquer thinner.

## REMOVING MILK PAINT

If you have an antique colored with red, green, black, or brown paint, and remover will not take it off, your antique might be finished with milk paint. Ordinary removers will not remove this finish. You need ammonia. Household ammonia works, but concentrated ammonia, if you can find it, works better. The problem with ammonia is its harsh fumes. You will need good ventilation with a cross draft to keep the ammonia fumes away from your face. Also, wear rubber gloves to protect hands.

To remove the milk paint, cover the item with ammonia. Keep it wet. Dip a piece of 2/0 steel wool in a pan full of ammonia and scrub the finish with the steel wool. Continue applying ammonia and scrubbing with steel wool until the finish comes off; this might take a half hour of soaking. When the finish is gone, clean the wood with water, rub it dry, and place it in a warm place for one or more days to dry.

Adding trisodium phosphate to ammonia will speed the removing process. Add equal parts of ammonia, T.S.P., and hot water (1/2 cup to 1 gallon of water).

If the wood is darkened by ammonia, it can be lightened by bleaching with oxalic acid (see Chapter 6, *Bleaching*).

# Chapter 3
# Gluing and clamping

When the finish on your project has been removed, check to see that the joints are tight. Rock the piece, twist it, put a mild strain on it. Any loose joints should be reglued.

Glue is the adhesive that holds loose joints or broken wood together. Properly joined, the glued area can be stronger than a nonbroken section.

Clamps, either commercial or homemade, can hold broken wood together until the glue dries. Figure 3-1 shows an assortment of clamps.

Do not use nails and screws to repair broken furniture. They soon loosen, often causing the surrounding wood to rot or split. Nails and screws can be used to hold glue blocks or broken pieces in place while the glue dries, but it is the glue that holds the joint together, not the nail.

The most important step when regluing is cleaning or scraping off the old glue. If glue is to hold properly, it must be absorbed into the wood. Old glue on the wood's surface prevents this absorption. New glue applied over old glue will not hold, a strain will easily loosen an improperly cleaned joint.

## SELECTING A GLUE

Consider the following qualities when selecting a glue:

- Premixes for convenience
- Has a long shelf life
- Does not harden in the container
- Dries in a reasonable time, but sets up slowly to give you time to apply the glue, assemble, and clamp
- Does not show a dark glue line when dry

**28** *Gluing and clamping*

**3-1** Use clamps to hold wood together while the glue dries.

Before gluing, it is important to know what kind of clamping to use and what drying temperature is required. Is the glue waterproof? If a mistake is made, can the hardened glue be softened and the item disassembled? Useful wood glues are shown in FIG. 3-2.

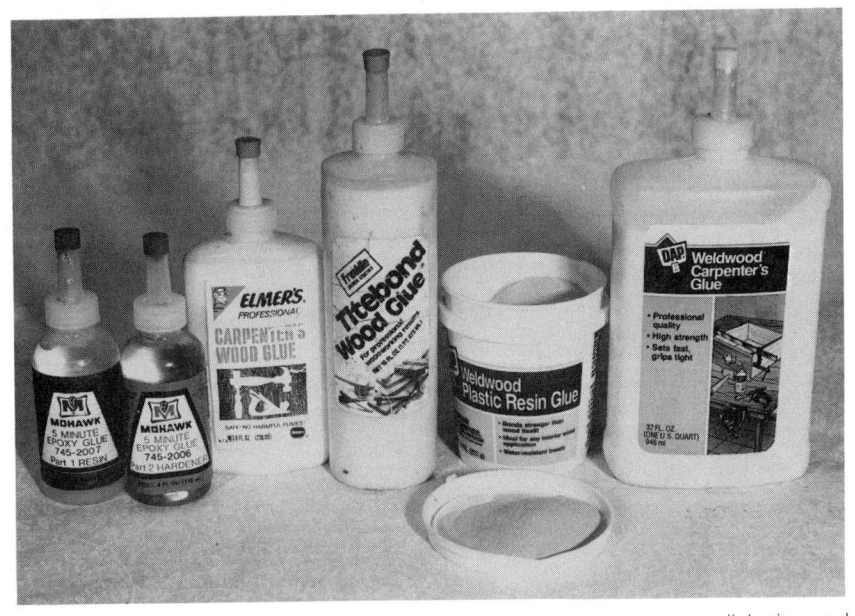

**3-2** Adhesives used to glue wood are (from left to right): fast-drying epoxy, aliphatic wood glue, water-resistant plastic resin glue, and another aliphatic glue.

### White glue (polyvinyl resin)

Elmers Glue All, in liquid form, can be used for furniture and household repairs and for gluing leather and paper. Use it on material that can absorb moisture. It has no visible glue line; it is not waterproof; it softens at 140 degrees; it sets up slowly and it dries in three hours at 70 degrees. Good for small projects.

### Yellow glue (aliphatic emulsion)

Tite Bond and Elmer's Carpenter Glue are excellent yellow glues to use for furniture construction and household repairs. Yellow glue is good for nonporous woods and hardboard that can absorb moisture. It leaves no visible glue line, dries fast with a strong bond, sets up in 2 to 3 hours at 70 degrees, and is moisture resistant.

### Powdered plastic resin glue

Weldwood and Borden's Cosco glue come in powder form and are mixed with water. Powdered plastic resin glue is good for furniture construction on material where moisture can be absorbed. It is practically waterproof; requires clean, good-fitting joints; must be used within 4 hours after mixing; dries in 10 hours with a strong bond; and requires tight clamping.

### Epoxy

Epoxy dries by the addition of a catalyst. It is an excellent glue to use to hold nonporous materials such as plastic, glass, metal, and ceramics. Epoxy comes in two separate containers; equal parts are mixed together. It is extremely strong and waterproof. Some brands dry in 5 minutes; others take 12 hours.

### Hide glue

Hide glue was used on antiques and new furniture until about 1950. This glue comes ready-mixed or in flake form. The flakes are liquefied by soaking in water and heated in a hot glue pot. When the glue cools, it hardens.

Museum conservators recommend hide glue for use on antiques. If a mistake is made when gluing, and it is necessary to change or correct the repair, the glued piece can be taken apart by soaking in warm water or vinegar without harming the item.

Use it on materials that can absorb moisture. It is not waterproof and can be removed with warm water or vinegar.

Because hide glue dries slowly, consider it when gluing veneers because it gives you ample time to position the veneer, move and slide it around, and apply clamps. Later, when dry, if it is necessary to remove the veneer, you can soften hide glue by soaking it in hot water or vinegar; the veneer will peel off.

### Resorcinol resin glue

Resorcinol resin glue comes in two parts: a liquid resin and powdered catalyst. The two parts are mixed together to form a strong waterproof glue. It can be used on exterior plywood, furniture, and boats. It dries in 8 hours.

### Recommendations

Aliphatic glue (Tite Bond or Elmer's Carpenters glue) is the glue I would recommend for gluing wood. It is strong, dries rapidly, and is reasonably water resistant.

Powdered plastic resin glue (Weldwood and Borden's Cosco) is the recommended glue for wood that will be exposed to considerable moisture. It is almost waterproof and very strong.

Resorcinol resin glue is recommended when you need a strong, completely waterproof glue.

## GLUING AND CLAMPING

Wood being glued should be at a room temperature of 70 degrees or higher. The surface to be glued, call it the *glue line*, must be free of all dirt and old glue. Glue that is being applied will not stick to old glue, oil, or dirt. Glue lines must be clean and make a good contact with one another.

Before applying glue, put each piece into place to ensure a proper fit, then disassemble. Apply glue to both surfaces; fit the pieces together. Remove all glue that squeezes from the joint using a rag wet with warm water.

Cover the glue line on both sides with wax paper. Place small blocks of wood on the wax paper and tighten the clamp over the wood blocks. Remove excess glue with a wet rag. The block of wood protects the furniture from being damaged by the clamp; wax paper keeps the wood block from being glued to the furniture (see FIG. 3-3).

Tighten the clamp, if the joint does not fit together properly, loosen the clamp and tap the joint with a rubber hammer to jar the wood into

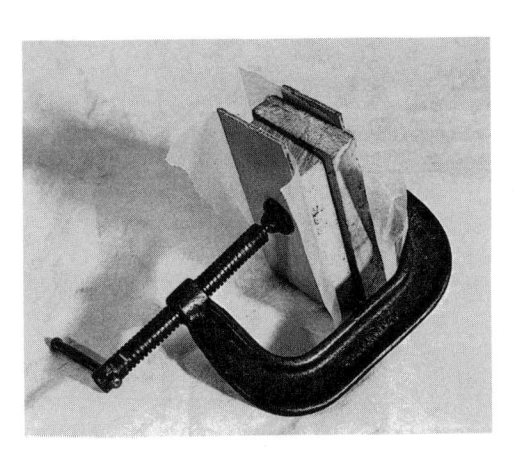

**3-3** To protect the wood from the metal clamps, place wood blocks between the clamp and project. Use wax paper under the blocks if glue is present.

place. Retighten the clamp but not too tight; you do not want all the glue to be squeezed from the joint. Again, clean off any glue that oozes out of the joint.

When possible, allow the project to dry overnight at a temperature of 70 degrees or higher. Keep the project level and align chairs and cases before they dry. Fit drawers to assure a proper fit. Figures 3-4 and 3-5 illustrate the use of different types of clamps.

Wax paper under the block of wood slows the glue's drying time. If a fast repair is required, use paper in place of wax paper. It will stick to the glue but can be removed with water or sanded off when the clamps are removed.

**3-4** Use adjustable pipe clamps to span wide surfaces.

## Drying time

- White glue, Elmer's (polyvinyl resin)—3 or more hours
- Yellow carpenter's glue (aliphatic)—3 or more hours
- Plastic resin (powdered)—10 hours
- Hide glue (animal flake)—12 hours
- Epoxy (two part)—5 minutes to 12 hours
- Resorcinol resin glue (powdered)—8 hours

All of these glues reach their maximum strength in about 12 hours at 70 degrees.

*Materials*

Glue

Rags

Warm water

Wood blocks (2" × 3" × 1/4")

Wax paper

Clamps—rubber bands, tourniquet, web clamps, C clamps, bar clamps, wood clamps (see FIG. 3-1)

Rubber mallet

*Application*

1. Clean off old glue, dirt, and oil from glue line.
2. Smooth surfaces to make solid contact with one another.
3. Assemble project to ensure that parts fit together properly.
4. Disassemble and apply a wet, even coat of glue to all surfaces being bonded.
5. Squeeze the joint together with clamps. Place wood blocks under the clamp's jaws; place wax paper under the wood blocks. Thick newspaper can be used under the tourniquet to protect the wood.
6. Quickly clean off all glue that is squeezed from the joints.
7. Square and align parts before glue dries.
8. Dry overnight.
9. Remove clamps and scrape or sand off any remaining glue.

**3-5** From top to bottom: a wooden screw clamp, an inexpensive rubber band clamp, and a rope tourniquet.

## REPAIRING DAMAGED WOOD

When gluing dowels and stretchers on chair and table legs, apply glue to the end of the dowel. Do not put glue in the hole the dowel fits into. If the hole is filled with glue, the dowel might not fit in.

Occasionally a loose leg on a table or chair cannot be disassembled because it would be damaged by being knocked apart. An effective way to tighten these joints is to drill a small hole into the underside of the joint where the loose pieces meet. Force glue into the hole with a squeeze bottle or a hypodermic needle. If glue can penetrate inside and around the loose joint, it will often be tightened when the glue hardens. Putty can be used to fill the small hole.

### Loose veneers

Carefully loosen and lift the loose veneer. Try to clean off any dirt or glue that is on the core wood under the veneer. When clean, force glue under the veneer. Use a thin blade to spread it evenly. To clamp, place wax paper over the break, then a smooth block of wood over the wax paper, then the clamp over the wood block. Tighten the clamp.

When loose veneer is being lifted off the core wood, if it splits or breaks off, do not be alarmed. When the pieces are reglued, you can match the broken edges together, and the break will be almost invisible. Never cut a veneer off; the cut edge can never be made to look natural. Better to break it off.

### Blisters in veneers

Slit the blister along the grain with a sharp razor blade. If the cut blister overlaps when it is pressed flat, trim off the excess veneer until it does lay flat. Next, heat the blister with a hot iron. The hide glue will soften and readhere when heated. If the old glue does not hold, force new glue under the blister and clamp. A heavy weight might be enough to hold it down. When the glue dries, if needed, fill the slit with putty, sand, stain, and refinish the surface.

If necessary, on a finished surface, after the blister is glued down, burn in the slit with a lacquer stick or puddle with sealer. Dry, sand, and again coat with finish.

### Surface cracks (glue sizing)

To repair small cracks in veneer or solid wood, rub white glue that has been thinned with water onto the cracked surface. Force the thin glue into the cracks with your fingers. Rub the glue back and forth across the cracks, pressing hard until the cracks are filled. Remove excess glue from the surface with a damp cloth. When dry, sand the surface smooth and refinish.

### Splits in solid wood

Split tabletops, table leaves, panels, and boards are not difficult to repair. Force the split open; clean out the dirt; force glue into the opening; and clamp. When the split is being forced open, it is possible that the wood might break in half. If this happens, try to keep the wood from coming completely apart. It will be easier to reglue if some of the wood is intact.

### Edge splits with the grain (Dutchmans)

Cracks that start on the edge of a board and run a short distance with the grain can be repaired by cutting into the split with a saw. Use a fine-tooth saw to carefully saw into and to the end of the split. Cut out a thin strip of matching wood, a *Dutchman*, on a table saw. Insert it into the saw cut, glue, sand when dry, and refinish.

Sounds scary, but it does work. The patch, when sanded and refinished, is often invisible.

### Oblique edge splits (against the grain)

Splits that take off on an angle from an edge can be doweled. Drill a small hole into the edge and across the crack. If possible, force glue into the crack. Drive a wood dowel covered with glue into the hole. Cut off the dowel at the edge of the board and sand smooth. When the top is refinished, the crack might be seen because it is cross-grain, but the dowel will keep the split from widening.

### Glue blocks

The small triangular or square blocks of wood that are glued to the underside of furniture are called *glue blocks*. They reinforce joints where two pieces of wood are joined at right angles, making the piece strong and rigid. Quality furniture is constructed with glue blocks.

### Wood plugs

Screws that are used to reinforce joints on the outside surface of chairs are often countersunk and covered with a wood plug or button. These plugs are used to hide screwheads. If the plug is made of the same wood as the chair, it can be invisible.

To tighten or take out a screw that has a plug over it the plug must be removed. A button plug overlaps the screw hole and can be removed by forcing a screwdriver or knife blade under its edge and prying it out. Wood plugs are more difficult to remove. They are flush with the surface and must be dug out with an awl or cut out with a drill. Turning a screw into the center of the plug will also force it out.

To replace the plug, cut a new one out of a wooden dowel, or use a button. Buttons and plugs are sold in lumber and hardware stores. Apply a little glue and tap them into place. A plug might need to be puttied, sanded, stained, and finished to match the surrounding finish.

## Screws

Screws are used to reinforce corner blocks that hold legs on tables and chairs. They strengthen chair arms and are used extensively on the inside of cabinets.

The problem with screws is they eventually work loose. Wood around the metal slowly rots away and the screws loosen. Screws are good to hold glue joints and glue blocks in place while the glue dries, but in the end, it is glue that holds the piece together, not the screw.

## Nails and staples

The only time a nail or staple should be used on furniture is to hold a glue block in place while the glue dries. Nails rapidly work loose, often split the wood when driven in, and have little holding strength. Do not use them.

# Chapter 4

# Filling dents and holes

*A* fast way to fill small holes and dents in wood is to use wood putty or wood dough. These heavy-bodied fillers dry fast, and resist shrinking. One type of putty has a tan or pine color, when this putty hardens it should match the natural tone of pine and light-colored woods.

Most putties will not absorb stain. When wood filled with putty is stained, the filler will not darken. Stain will darken the surrounding wood but not the putty; putty retains its light color and will be a light spot under the finish. To remedy this problem, dry color or oil color can be added to the filler, matching it to the color of the stained wood.

Some putties have colors added to them, such as walnut, mahogany, oak, cedar, and many more wood colors. One type of putty absorbs stain when it hardens, and another type has color added and also absorbs stain—but both of these fillers have a problem. Because there is no way to control the amount of stain that is absorbed, they usually become too dark.

Matching the color of wood with putty can be difficult. When using colored putty, you must anticipate how the putty will look, not only on bare wood, but how the wood will look with a stain on it. Then you must appropriately color the filler or buy precolored putty with the correct color added. You might have to hide the miscolored fill spot by brushing color over the filler, simulating the surrounding grain pattern and color. An assortment of wood fillers are pictured in FIG. 4-1.

## APPLYING PUTTY

To apply putty or wood dough, press it into the hole with a small putty knife. Apply filler to the hole only, do not smear it around (FIG. 4-2). Putty will fill wood pores wherever it is rubbed. Later, when finished over, the

**4-1** Putties are used to fill dents and holes in wood.

**4-2** Press putty into the hole, not the surrounding wood.

surface where putty was smeared will not look the same as the surrounding wood. The puttied area will be smooth and slick, while the adjoining area will be porous.

When putty is used to fill deep holes, it might shrink when dry and need a second application. Overnight drying is recommended for large or deep holes.

*Materials*

Putty:
- Wood colors added; for example, walnut, mahogany, etc.
- Natural without color
- Lacquer-soluble
- Water-soluble
- Putty with a catalyst added

Colors to add to putty:
- Oil color
- Dry powder color

Solvents to thin putty:

Read putty manufacturer's directions
- Lacquer thinner
- Water

Putty knife (1-inch wide blade)

Sandpaper (60, 100, 150, or 180 grit depending on the condition of the surface)

*Application*

1. If necessary, color the putty to match the color of the wood when it is stained.
2. Press the putty into the hole with a small putty knife. Do not smear it around.
3. Allow the putty to dry hard.
4. If the first application shrinks, apply a second coat.
5. When dry, sand smooth.

## PUTTY USED ON BARE WOOD

There are a variety of fillers that are used to fill dents and mold small missing parts on wood.

### Wood dough

Wood dough is used to fill large holes in wood. Thin it with lacquer thinner. When soft, color it with stain; it cannot be stained when it hardens. Shallow holes dry in one hour; deep holes need multiple coats and must dry overnight. Two brands are Duratite Wood Dough and Plastic Wood. Some of these putties have wood colors added.

### Surfacing putty

Surfacing putty is a white-colored putty that is used to fill small holes in wood or metal. Surfacing putty cannot be colored with a stain after it hardens. Thin it with lacquer thinner. Because surfacing putty is white, use it only on wood or metal that is to be painted with a solid color. One brand is Duratite Surfacing Putty.

### Automotive body putty

This polyester filler is used by automobile painters to fill dents on cars. A catalyst is added to make this product harden. It dries in one-half hour or less. It has excellent adhesion to wood or metal, and dries extremely hard. Automotive body putty is good to fill large holes or to make and shape missing parts. It does not shrink. Sand or cut it to shape before it completely hardens.

There are problems with automotive body putty. It dries very hard, which makes it difficult to sand when it fully hardens. It is usually colored blue or gray. It does not accept stain when hardened. Finally, it must be painted or grained over.

### Sanding dust

Mix sanding dust from the wood you are going to putty with glue and apply it to the hole. When the glue dries, sand level. Sanding dust is not a good putty, and it cannot be stained over. Finishes also do not adhere well to glue.

### Water putty

There are two types of water putty: dry powder and premixed.

## PUTTY USED ON FINISHES

The following fillers are used to fill dents and scratches in finishes.

### Crayons

Colored crayons can be used to make temporary repairs to dents in finishes. Crayon is not a good putty, but it is easy to use, easy to find, and easy to remove. Simply melt or press the proper-colored crayon into the dent, then rub off the excess wax with a rag dampened with paint thinner.

### Lacquer

Lacquer can be dripped into dents in lacquer finishes. After it dries, apply it again if it shrinks, and dry it again. Continue this process until the dent is filled. When the lacquer dries, rock hard, sand it level with the surrounding finish. After sanding, rub the entire surface with fine steel wool, or pumice and water, to remove the scratches left in the finish by the sandpaper. If the surface still does not look good, spray the patched spot and entire top with a satin or gloss lacquer.

## Wax putty sticks

Soft wax sticks come in many furniture colors. They are made to be rubbed into dents and cracks in finishes. Although the wax never hardens, some brands can be finished over. They can also be used to color scratches by rubbing them over the scratch, leaving just enough color behind to hide it. Remove excess wax left around the hole or scratch with fine steel wool, or rub it off using a cloth dampened with paint thinner. Because wax does not harden, it is not permanent and can be easily removed.

## Lacquer sticks

Lacquer sticks also are called *shellac sticks* and *burn-in sticks*. These hard, brittle fillers are called sticks because of their long and slender shape. These fillers are used by finishers to fill small holes in wood or dents in finishes. When heated, the lacquer stick softens. When cool, it hardens. It is softened with a hot flat blade called a *burn-in iron*; special heaters are used to heat the blade.

Melt a small amount of filler out of the lacquer stick with the hot burn-in iron and carefully place it into the hole. Use the flat hot blade to carefully smooth this filler over the hole and blend it into the finish. When the filler hardens, which only takes a few seconds, sand and rub the filler smooth. If the color of the patch is not right, grain it with color and coat the surface with finish. Figure 4-3 shows an assortment of fillers used to fill dents in finishes.

Lacquer sticks are available in a wide variety of furniture colors. Different colored sticks can be melted together to match any wood or finish tone. This patching method takes considerable practice and skill when used to fill holes in finishes. The hot iron used to melt and smooth the burn-in stick can easily burn and blister finishes. Finishers call this process of patching *burning in*. It is invaluable to finishers who work for factories and furniture stores where touch-up repairs are an important part of their work (see Chapter 15, *Touching Up*).

**4-3** From top to bottom: burn-in sticks, wax putty touch-up sticks, and crayons.

# Chapter 5
# Sanding

*P*rior to finishing, new wood must be sanded smooth to remove dents, scratches, and rough sandpaper marks. Furniture that is being refinished does not always require excessive sanding. If the wood has not been damaged, scratched, or dented, all that is needed is a light sanding with 180-grit sandpaper to remove loose wood fibers raised in the removing process. A light sanding will also save any stain or filler that is in the wood, and considerable work. Sanding materials are shown in FIG. 5-1.

## SANDING ANTIQUES

When sanding antiques to save the patina, sand the wood lightly with fine 280-grit sandpaper. This sanding removes wood burrs that could snag or scratch. Do not sand off dents and scratches. Do not sandpaper turnings on legs and arms; there might be lathe marks on them. These marks are desirable and should be preserved. If they need smoothing, use steel wool.

### Patina

The old look wood has acquired over the years is called *patina*. It is an accumulation of dirt, grime, and wear from cleaning and use. Old finishes become darker and richer in color, unfinished wood can turn from an amber yellow maple to a smokey brown. This patina should not be destroyed; when gone, it cannot be replaced. Patina can only be obtained through age.

The finish on a valuable museum-quality antique should not be removed. If the finish has been removed, the patina in the wood must not be destroyed by sanding. Removing the finish or sanding off the patina that is in the wood will reduce the value of the antique.

**5-1** Sandpaper and soft-bottom sandpaper blocks.

## Signs of wear on antiques

Signs of wear on an antique can include:

- Slightly rounded and dented edges
- Dulled carvings
- Shrinking of wood against the grain
- Warped leaves
- Stretchers on chairs and tables worn by shoes
- Drawer sides worn on their bottom
- Candle burns on ladder-back chairs and tilt-top tables.

These signs of wear attest to the authenticity of the piece. They are part of their character, characteristics that should be preserved.

## SANDPAPER SELECTION

There are several symbols printed on the back of a sheet of sandpaper. Each has a meaning and tells something about that piece of sandpaper.

- *Aluminum oxide, garnet, emery*, etc., designates the type of abrasive glued on the paper.
- The numbers 60, 100, 600, etc., tells the grit size, or size of the abrasive particle.
- *Open* or *closed coat* is the density of abrasive particles on the paper.
- *Wet* or *dry* means the paper is waterproof.
- The letters *A, B, C*, etc., tells the weight or strength of paper or cloth to which the abrasive particles are glued.

On the back of the sandpaper is printed the type of abrasive particle that is glued to the paper and for what it is best. Some abrasives are made to sand wood; others sand finishes, metal, or plastics.

### Abrasives used to sand wood

*Aluminum oxide* is made of bauxite coke and iron filings. This abrasive is hard and tough, cuts fast, is long lasting. It is good for hand and machine sanding and is the best abrasive to use when sanding wood. It also is used on wet or dry paper.

*Garnet* is reddish brown in color, the same natural mineral as the semiprecious jewel. Garnet is good for hand-sanding wood and light machine sanding. It is not as long lasting as aluminum oxide because it wears out faster.

*Flint*, or white quartz, looks like sand. It can be used for simple hand-sanding. Flint is not a durable abrasive. It does not cut well, nor does it last long. Do not use flint sandpaper.

### Abrasives used to sand metal and finishes

*Silicone carbide* is black in color and made of bauxite coke and iron filings. It cuts fast and is long-lasting. It is used on wet or dry sandpaper to sand finishes, metal, and plastic.

*Emery* is black in color and made of iron oxide and corundum. It is used to sand metal. This abrasive is usually glued to a cloth backing for flexibility and strength.

*Free cut*, or *white zinc stearate*, is a white coating applied over the abrasive on sandpaper. It acts as a lubricant to reduce particle clogging, or sanding debris that fill the area between the abrasive particles and make the abrasive ineffective.

### Sandpaper grit numbers

Abrasives used on sandpaper come in large pieces that are crushed or broken apart. The broken particles are sifted into grit size by passing them over a series of accurately woven silk screens. The number of openings on these screens per square inch range from many hundred to just a few.

The number of openings per linear inch is used to designate grit size. Grits that pass through a screen with 80 openings per linear inch are called *grit size 80*; grits that pass through a screen with 400 holes per linear inch are called *400 grit*. The smaller the opening, the smaller the particle and the larger the grit size number.

Spacing or density of the abrasive particles on sandpaper determines the use of the paper.

- *Open coat* is used to sand wood. The abrasive particles cover only 50 to 70 percent of the paper's surface. The wide spacing helps prevent sanding dust from clogging the abrasive particles. It is fast-cutting and requires less pressure. Abrasives commonly used are garnet, aluminum oxide, and flint.

- *Closed coat* is used to sand finishes, metal, and plastic. The abrasive particles are placed very close together. Used on wet or dry sandpaper.

- *Wet or dry* sandpaper has abrasive particles that are glued to the paper with waterproof glue. They do not come off when used with water, and can be used to sand finishes, metal, and plastics. The abrasives are usually silicon carbide or emery. Water or paint thinner can be used as a lubricant.

Water serves three purposes when used with wet sanding:

1. Water keeps the abrasive particles from being filled with sanding debris.
2. Water acts as a lubricant, allowing the paper to move smoothly across a surface.
3. Water keeps the sandpaper and finish cool.

The weight, strength, and flexibility of the sandpaper backing is designated by letters A through X.

- Paper—letter "A" is lightweight finishing paper for hand sanding; letters "C" and "D" are intermediate weight, cabinet paper for hand and light machine sanding; and letter "E" is strong heavy paper for machine and belt use.
- Cloth—letter "J", jeans cloth, is lightweight and flexible; and letter "X", drills cloth, is durable and strong.
- Combination—paper and cloth.
- Fiber—rag stock paper, disc and drum.

## Sandpaper grit size

**60 and 80 grit**  Coarse sandpaper for first sanding on rough new wood or wood that is deeply dented and scratched. After the wood has been sanded with 60-grit sandpaper, you must sand with 100-grit sandpaper to remove scratches made by the coarse 60 grit.

**100 and 120 grit**  Medium-coarse sandpaper used to remove scratches left in the wood by 60- and 80-grit sandpaper. Use it for first sanding on moderately scratched wood. Leaves sandpaper scratch marks that can be removed with 180- and 150-grit sandpaper. Can help hardwood absorb more stain, thus darkening it.

**180 and 150 grit**  Fine sandpaper used to remove scratches left by 100- or 120-grit sandpaper. Use it for first and last sanding on wood with minor scratches.

**280 and 240 grit**  Very fine sandpaper. Use it to obtain an extra smooth surface on wood. With caution, it makes sanding heavy coats of sanding sealer easier but must be used carefully because it cuts through sealer quickly.

**400 to 600 grit**  Extra fine wet or dry sandpaper. Use it to sand finishes. On level surfaces, use a sandpaper block with the paper and water as a lubricant. Good to sand lacquer, varnish, urethane, and automotive finishes. Also can be used to sand plastics and metal. Wet or dry paper will smooth a lacquer finish faster if paint thinner is used in place of water as the lubricant.

*Materials*

Sandpaper for wood, open coat:

    Coarse—60 and 80 grit

    Medium-coarse—100 and 120 grit

    Fine—150 and 180 grit

    Extra fine—240 or 280 grit

    Sandpaper block about 3 × 5 × 1 inches to sand flat surfaces

    Blackboard eraser for concave surfaces

Sandpaper for finishes, closed coat:

    320, 400, and 600 grit

    Paint thinner or water

    Sandpaper block for flat surfaces

    Rags to clean off water or paint thinner

Power hand sanders

Straight-line sander

Orbital sander

Belt sanders for badly damaged or rough solid new wood; never use on veneered surfaces or antiques

## PROPER SANDING TECHNIQUES

To hand sand a flat surface, tear a full sheet of sandpaper into four equal pieces. Wrap one piece around a sandpaper block. Note: place the soft bottom side of the block toward the surface being sanded. Hold the paper tightly in place on both sides of the block with your fingers. Apply moderate pressure with your hand. Apply enough downward pressure to make the sandpaper move freely and cut, but do not restrict its movement across the surface.

    Start in one corner; sand that spot *with the grain* 10 or more times using about 12-inch strokes. When that spot has been sanded, move over and sand the space next to it, slightly overlapping, and sand it 10 or more times. Continue sanding until the entire surface has been sanded evenly. Then, with long strokes, sand with the grain all the way across the surface. Sand from one edge to the other without stopping until all the small sanded spots have been blended, FIG. 5-2. If you used a coarse sandpaper, sand the wood again using a finer grit sandpaper to remove the coarse sandpaper scratches.

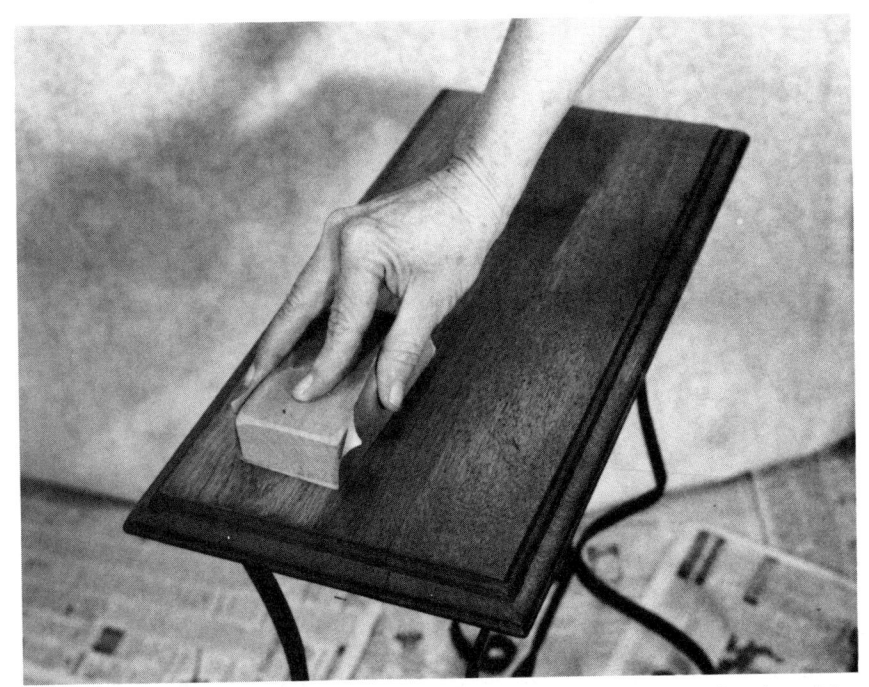

**5-2** On flat surfaces, use a soft-bottom sandpaper block and sand in the direction of the grain.

## Sanding hints

Sand one small area at a time, overlapping when moving to the next spot; then sand evenly across the total surface. Do not push sandpaper over edges; sand up to the edge and stop. Do not sand too long in one spot or sand through veneers.

To sand out a deep dent, use a sandpaper block. Sand the dent and a large area around the dent. If you only sand the dent, you will put a deep concave groove in the surface.

Sand hard open-pored wood, such as oak, ash, and pecan, at a slight angle to the grain. Although not a hardwood, fir should also be sanded at an angle.

Do not round edges; but if they are sharp, sand them lightly. Sand curved surfaces by hand, FIG. 5-3. Avoid sanding over bulges on table and chair turnings; you do not want to flatten them. Instead, rub them with steel wool.

A blackboard eraser used as a sanding block is excellent to sand concave surfaces.

To check the surface after sanding, wet the wood with paint thinner. Scratches and dents missed when sanding will appear on the wet surface. When the wood is stained, it will show any sanding errors such as rough sandpaper scratches, cross-grain scratches, unevenly sanded areas, and dents. If these rough spots are unacceptable, resand the surface and restain.

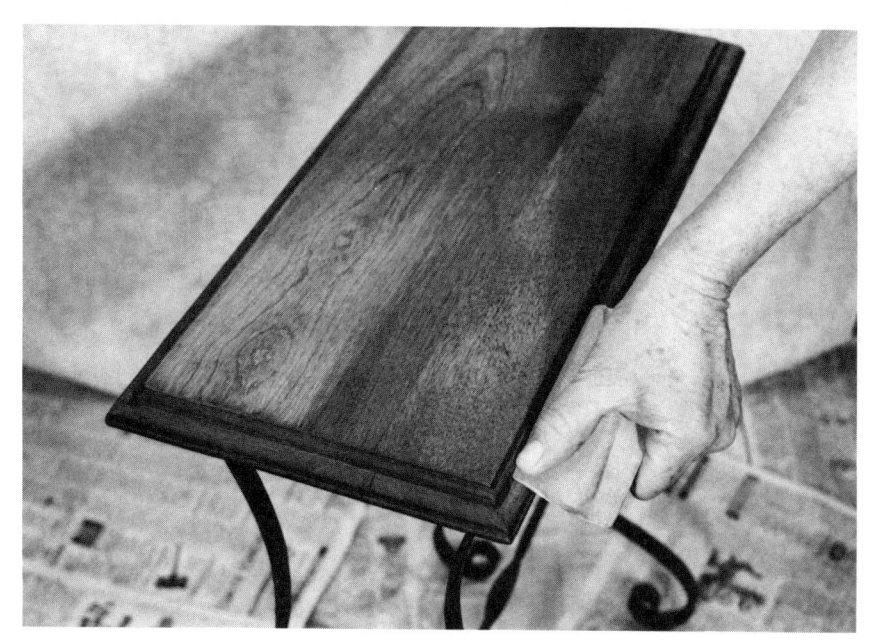

**5-3** Sand curved surfaces by hand.

Hardwoods that do not darken when stained will darken if, prior to staining, they are sanded with 100-grit sandpaper. This coarse sandpaper leaves small scratches in the wood that absorbs extra stain.

## SANDING SAFETY

A byproduct of sanding wood is sanding dust, small particles of wood cut off in the sanding process. These wood particles float around you and your project. Most of it ends up in your nose, plugging it and making your head stuffy. To avoid breathing this dust and coating your nose, wear an inexpensive dust mask. It looks like a surgeon's mask, is lightweight, and has a rubber band to hold it in place.

Try to sand in an area that has good cross-ventilation to carry the dust away. Sand outside when using power sanders. They can make a lot of dust that will cover you and your work area. A fan placed in a window or door will help move the dust away from you.

## SANDING TOOLS AND MACHINES

Certain tools and electric sanders will make sanding easier and faster. There are also a few tools and machines that should not be used.

### Sandpaper block

A sandpaper block is used to sand flat surfaces. Wrap the sandpaper around a block; hold it in your hand, and push it back and forth across the surface. By using a block, the total area of the sandpaper comes in contact with the surface being sanded. This utilizes the paper better and ensures that the wood surface is sanded even and level.

The bottom of the sandpaper block must be soft and spongy to conform to the contour of the surface being sanded. A soft bottom allows hard particles that might be loose on the wood to press up into the soft material on the bottom of the block, rather than be pushed down into the wood to cause scratches.

If you make a sandpaper block out of wood, glue a felt or cork pad to its bottom. Make the block about 3 inches wide, 5 inches long, and 1 inch thick. Glue a thick piece of felt to the block. A blackboard eraser works well, as does a rubber block; they both have soft bottoms. A plain wood block without a soft bottom can damage soft wood.

## Electric hand sanders

Vibrator and orbital sanders are excellent tools that speed the sanding of level surfaces. Figure 5-4 shows three different sanding machines. *Straight-line sanders* have pads that cut with the grain. The *orbital sander* has a pad that makes small circles as it cuts (FIG. 5-5). When you have finished sanding with an orbital sander, you must remove the small circles left on the wood. This is done by hand sanding with the grain, using the same grit sandpaper that was used on the machine. These circles are hard to see, but they are there; If they are not sanded off, they will appear when the wood is stained.

Some sanders are orbital and straight line. They make circles but, by

**5-4** Electric sanders (from left to right): a palm sander, a belt sander, and an orbital sander.

**5-5** An orbital hand sander.

turning a switch, become straight-line sanders. Use the orbital to cut rough wood because it cuts faster. Then turn the key for straight-line final sanding to remove the circles. High-speed orbital sanders leave less noticeable circles.

## Belt sanders

Belt sanders are powerful sanders that cut fast and deep. They are best used to level rough new wood. Caution is required when using a belt sander on furniture. If not handled properly, the sander will cut deep grooves into the wood surface.

When operating the sander, hold it tightly. Lower it onto the wood heel first. Move it back and forth and straight with the grain or at a slight angle on oak, ash, or fir. Avoid sanding over edges. My advice is to not use them except to smooth rough new wood.

## Scrapers

There are a multitude of scrapers: hand planes, broken glass, flat springs, and hook scrapers. They come in all sizes and shapes. Basically, they are pushed or pulled across the wood surface to peel off a strip of wood with each stroke. Scrapers can leave concave grooves and gouges in the surface. Because of their potential for gouging, do not use them on a fine piece of furniture. Only use scrapers on rough or badly damaged wood, never on antiques if you wish to preserve the patina.

## Cleaning dirty sandpaper

Sandpaper is often thrown away long before the abrasive particles are worn out. Sandpaper is expensive. To make it last longer, blow off dust that builds up between the abrasive particles. Use an air hose or clean it with a stiff brush. Remove embedded finish particles on wet or dry sandpaper by soaking it in lacquer thinner. Do not use closed-coat or wet or dry paper on wood. The abrasive particles will immediately be clogged with wood dust and the sandpaper will become worthless.

Use open-coat sandpaper to sand wood. The abrasive particles are spaced far apart. When the open spaces between the particles fill up with dust, tap the paper sharply or brush it clean with a stiff brush.

### Steel wool

Steel wool is an important finishing material that is as useful to a finisher as sandpaper. Steel wool is an abrasive that is made of fine strands of metal that are rolled into small hand-sized pads (FIG. 5-6). The pads are packaged in sleeves of 16 or packages of 8.

Use steel wool to smooth wood, to help remove finishes, to smooth finishes between coats, and when used with a lubricant, to hand rub finishes. Fine grades of steel wool do not cut, instead they burnish the surface being rubbed and roll over high spots rather than cut through them. There is less chance of rubbing through finishes when steel wool is used as a final rubbing abrasive.

| Grade | Texture | Use |
|-------|---------|-----|
| 0000 | Super fine | For cleaning finishes and rubbing down final coat of finish |
| 000 | Extra fine | Use to smooth finishes between coats |
| 00 | Fine | Use to smooth wood and to dull rub finishes |
| 0 | Medium fine | For finish removal and smoothing wood |
| 1 | Medium | For finish removal |

**5-6** Grades and uses of steel wool.

# Chapter 6
# Bleaching

Occasionally it is necessary to use bleach to lighten wood. It is not used often, but it is indispensable when needed. There are some bleaches that will burn your skin and eyes, so use bleach with caution. It is important to carefully follow the instructions printed on the container.

Bleach is used to:

- Lighten the natural color of wood when the wood is too dark.
- Bleach out the original stain color that was applied by the finisher.
- Remove dark circles, spots, water stains, and ink spots.
- Lighten wood darkened by lye or ammonia removers.

Bleach will not lighten wood burned by cigarettes or fire, nor will it remove lamp black graining on antiques. These blemishes can only be removed by sanding. Bleaching materials are pictured in FIG. 6-1.

## PREPARING TO BLEACH

Before using bleach, it is important to follow these instructions and the instructions on the bleach container.

- When using a hydrogen peroxide two-part bleach, you must protect your hands and eyes and wear rubber gloves. Wash off any bleach that comes in contact with your skin or eyes with water.
- The surface being bleached must be clean and free of finish, dirt, and oil. Sand the wood before you bleach the wood.
- When the bleaching process is completed, clean the wood with water, then neutralize the surface with vinegar. If the bleach is not thoroughly removed and neutralized, it will lighten stain that is applied over it.

## 52   Bleaching

- After the bleached wood has dried, usually overnight, lightly sand it with 280-grit sandpaper to remove wood fibers that puff up during bleaching. Sand lightly because the bleached surface is thin. Hard sanding will remove the light bleached surface and expose the darker under wood.

**6-1**   An assortment of wood bleaches (from left to right): Clorox, a mild bleach; oxalic acid; vinegar used as a neutralizer; and a two-part bleach.

## CHOOSING THE PROPER BLEACH

It is important to know which bleach to use on your project. Each bleach does a specific job.

### Clorox laundry bleach (sodium hypochlorite)

Clorox is a mild bleach that can be used to remove ink stains and stains put into the wood by a finisher. Clorox does not usually lighten wood.

Before bleaching, remove any finish, clean the wood, and sand the surface smooth. Work outside in direct sunlight. Clorox will not bleach without help from the sun.

Apply the bleach with a brush full strength as it comes from the container. Keep the wood wet for about 15 minutes; then wash the bleach off with water.

When clean, set the wood aside to dry overnight. When dry, sand it lightly with 280-grit sandpaper. Remember that a bleached surface is thin, and it is easy to sand through to the dark wood under the bleach.

*Materials*

Clorox

Brush

Water

Sunlight

Plastic container

Rags

280-grit sandpaper

*Application*

1. Pour Clorox into a plastic pail.
2. Apply to clean, sanded wood with a sponge, rag, or paintbrush.
3. Soak for 15 minutes *in the sun*.
4. Wash off with water.
5. Dry with rags.
6. Set aside to dry for two days.
7. Lightly sand puffed wood fibers with 280-grit sandpaper.

## Oxalic acid

Oxalic acid is a mild bleach. It is excellent to remove dark rings and black spots in wood that were caused by water. It also lightens wood that has been darkened by lye or ammonia removers.

Oxalic acid is a crystal that is dissolved in hot water. For large jobs, mix 1/2 pound of oxalic acid to 1 quart of hot water. For small jobs, mix 1 ounce of oxalic acid to 1 cup of hot water.

To lighten wood darkened by a lye or ammonia remover or to take out stains, apply the solution to the entire surface.

To remove black spots and rings (water spots), apply a wet paste solution of oxalic acid to the black spots. If the acid crystals dry before the wood is lightened or the black spots are removed, add more water to the crystals. On softwood, the dark spots are often removed in a few minutes. On hardwood, you might need to keep the wood wet with the acid solution for an hour or more.

When the black spots are removed, and to be sure the top is evenly bleached, coat the entire top with the acid solution. After the top is lightened, wash away the crystals with water, then neutralize the bleach by washing the wood with white vinegar. Allow the wet wood to dry for one day; then sand *lightly* with 280-grit sandpaper. Be careful because the bleached surface is thin and easy to sand through.

When applying oxalic acid, wear rubber gloves. Avoid breathing the fumes, especially when mixing with warm water.

Vinegar washed over a bleached surface neutralizes any remaining acid. If the acid is not neutralized, it will bleach and lighten stain that is later applied to the wood.

Look for oxalic acid crystals in paint and hardware stores.

*Materials*

Oxalic acid crystals or premixed oxalic acid

Plastic container

Hot water

Brush or sponge

Vinegar

280-grit sandpaper

*Application*

1. Remove old finish and sand the wood.
2. Dissolve oxalic acid crystals in hot water; mix in a plastic container (1-ounce acid to 1 cup water).
3. Apply to dark water spots. When the black spot disappears, apply to the entire surface with a brush or rubber sponge.
4. Allow the acid to remain wet on the surface until the spot disappears.
5. When bleaching is completed, clean the surface with water, let dry.
6. Neutralize the bleach by washing with white vinegar.
7. Wipe clean and dry for one day.
8. Lightly sand raised wood fibers with 280-grit sandpaper.

## Hydrogen peroxide

Hydrogen peroxide is a powerful bleach that removes the natural color from wood, turning it white. It also removes stains applied by a finisher. Peroxide bleach is sold in paint and hardware stores. It comes in two containers, labeled container #1 and container #2, or container "A" and container "B."

To use this product, read and follow the instructions carefully. This is a powerful bleach that will burn unprotected skin. The mixing instructions vary from one manufacturer to another. One might instruct you to mix equal parts from bottle "A" and "B" together in a glass or ceramic bowl; then apply it to the wood. Another brand of bleach might tell you to apply their bleach from one bottle onto the wood; then after a certain time has passed to apply a coat from their second bottle. The method of application varies from brand to brand. Follow manufacturer's instructions carefully. Figures 6-2 and 6-3 shows the use and effect of this bleach.

When using a peroxide bleach, wear rubber gloves to protect your hands. If any bleach splashes on your skin, wash it off immediately with water.

After you have finished bleaching and have cleaned the bleach from

**6-2** A two-part bleach.

**6-3** The dark walnut board is lightened after the bleach is applied.

the wood, following the manufacturer's instructions, give the wood a final vinegar wash. This guarantees that all the bleach is neutralized.

Set the item aside for one day to dry before sanding lightly with 280-grit sandpaper. Be careful not to sand through the thin bleached surface or to breath sanding dust from a bleached surface.

*Materials*

Hydrogen peroxide two-part bleach

Glass or ceramic container

Sponge

Rags

Vinegar

Rubber gloves and eye protection

280-grit sandpaper

*Application*

1. Follow the manufacturer's instructions.
2. Finish by neutralizing the bleached surface with vinegar.
3. Protect hands and skin from splashed bleach. Wear rubber gloves and wear an eye shield.
4. Lightly sand off raised wood fibers.

## REMOVING RED STAINS

The most difficult stain to remove from wood is red aniline dye used to make red mahogany. These red stains penetrate deeply into the wood. They are difficult to sand off or to bleach out. It might be necessary to use several bleaches to remove them. Trisodium phosphate (T.S.P.), Clorox, and if necessary, a two-part hydrogen peroxide bleach.

Wash the surface with a mixture of 1 cup T.S.P. to 1 gallon of water. Flood and scrub the surface, washing away as much red color as will come out. Dry the wood and apply Clorox laundry bleach full strength, again flooding the wood and keeping it wet. To make the bleach work, apply it in the sun; it will not work without sunlight.

If the red has been removed, clean the piece with water and neutralize the surface with vinegar. If the wood is still too red or dark, you can lighten it further by applying a two-part hydrogen peroxide bleach, following the manufacturer's directions. Used individually, the T.S.P. and Clorox are not very effective, but they work well if used in sequence.

*Materials*

T.S.P. (trisodium phosphate)

Clorox laundry bleach

Sunlight

Water

Scrub brush

Two-part hydrogen peroxide bleach (if necessary)

Protect hands and eyes from bleach

280-grit sandpaper

*Application*

1. Thoroughly clean and sand the wood.
2. Mix 1 cup T.S.P. with 1 gallon of water.
3. Apply dissolved T.S.P. to wood and scrub.
4. Wipe off T.S.P. and apply Clorox to the wood in full sunlight. Keep wet for 15 minutes.
5. Clean with water and dry for two days.
6. Sand of raised wood fibers with 280-grit sandpaper.
7. If still not light enough, use a commercial two-part bleach. See the instructions on how to use hydrogen peroxide bleach.

## MISCELLANEOUS BLEACHES

1. Sodium hypochlorite crystals
2. Chlorinated lime—2 cups to 1 quart water. Good on walnut. Neutralize with vinegar or borax.
3. Hydrosulphite 10 percent—neutralize with vinegar.
4. Sodium perborate—neutralize with vinegar.
5. Potassium permanganate for the first coat; sodium bisulphate for the second coat.
6. Bleaching with opaque white lacquer.
7. Imitation graining that does not come off with remover or bleach must be sanded off.
8. If black spots appear on walnut or oak after bleaching, remove with sodium bisulphate—6 ounces to 1 gallon of water. Probably caused by steel wool on the wood.
9. Use hydrogen peroxide to remove ink stains.

# Chapter 7

# Staining

*Y*ou are finally arriving at a step in the finishing process where you can actually see progress being made. Wood that has had its finish removed and has been sanded probably does not look very good. You might think that finishing is not much fun, especially the removing and sanding. Cheer up! When your project is stained, its wood is brightened, the color of the grain is brought out, and you can begin to feel that progress is being made. That ugly old thing is going to look great (FIG. 7-1).

## TO STAIN OR NOT TO STAIN

I have heard this discussed many times. To settle this argument, my advice is to visit a furniture store or to look at the furniture in your home. You will see wood that has color. The following woods—maple, birch, and pine—are light colored, almost white; They are usually stained, as are oak, ash, and pecan. Dark walnut and mahogany woods are also stained. Factories go to considerable time and expense to stain, glaze, and shade these woods to uniform their color and make them more attractive. How often have you seen a factory-finished piece that is natural, except in an unfinished or natural wood store? The natural color of most wood is bland and uninteresting. Even the wood on your antique was stained way back when.

There are some who like their wood natural with no stain at all, and there are woods that do look good without stain. There are others who want their wood dark, and that is all right. What is important is what you like. I am in the middle, not wanting to obscure or make the wood look muddy, but wanting enough stain to enhance the natural grain and color of the wood.

**7-1** Stains and staining equipment.

## WHEN TO USE STAINS

Woods that lack beauty in color or grain should be stained. Antiques that have mellowed and darkened with age have a patina and might not need stain. Stain is needed:

- To bring out the beauty of the grain design and give life to the grain.
- To color wood when the wood has no natural beauty in color or grain.
- When the wood has faded or grayed, to add color and bring it back to life.
- When the wood was previously stained, and you want to replace the original color.
- To unify the color. If the piece is made of several types of wood, the lighter pieces are stained to match darker parts.
- To change the color of wood; to make mahogany or maple look like walnut, or walnut to look like mahogany.

## ANILINE STAINS

Aniline color is a term loosely used to indicate coal tar dyes or derivatives. Aniline dyes are excellent colors. They give bright vivid colors, penetrate deeply, are color-fast, and do not muddy the wood. Anilines can be brushed or sprayed on wood. Anilines can be difficult for beginners but are favored by experienced finishers.

Powdered aniline comes in small packages that are mixed with a solvent. Aniline is also used in ready-mixed stains that are sold in paint and hardware stores.

Because aniline stain penetrates deeply, the color must be correct. Once in the wood, aniline is difficult to remove. If the color is not the right shade, it might be necessary to bleach or sand it off. Before using an aniline stain, test the color on an obscure part of the wood.

Aniline powdered stains are not easily found in paint stores. They can be purchased from furniture finishing supply dealers through the mail.

### Aniline powder stains

There are three types of aniline powders. Each is made to be mixed with a different solvent, and each behaves differently.

**Water-soluble aniline stains** The powder is mixed with boiling water, about 1 ounce of stain to 1 quart of water. It is applied evenly with a brush or spray gun to wood that is slightly damp. Because water in the stain raises the grain, the surface is lightly sanded after the stain dries.

Care must be taken not to sand through the thin stained surface or to sand while the stain is wet. Aside from the problem of raised grain, water-soluble aniline is the best of the anilines. It gives the clearest colors, without fading or bleeding into finish coats.

**Alcohol-soluble aniline stains** Alcohol-soluble stain is dissolved in denatured alcohol. This stain is difficult to apply. The alcohol evaporates quickly, making it hard to apply evenly with a rag or brush without streaking. A spray gun is the best method of application. This stain is nongrain raising, so it is not necessary to sand the wood after staining; it does not raise the grain or bleed into top coats.

**Oil-soluble aniline dye** Oil-soluble aniline powders mix with many oil-base solvents—benzol, toluol, lacquer thinner, and paint thinner. This is the easiest of the anilines to use.

Oil-soluble anilines dry slowly, giving more time to apply them evenly. They do not raise the grain, so no aftersanding is necessary. It bleeds somewhat into the finish, and it is not light fast. These stains can be applied with a rag, brush, or spray.

For the beginner, I suggest you leave the powdered aniline to the professionals and use oil colors. If you do use an aniline, use one that is oil soluble.

## OIL STAINS

*Pigmented oil stains* are finely ground colors that have been mixed with linseed oil and thinned with mineral spirit. They are applied to wood with a rag, brush, or spray gun, allowed to soak in for a few minutes, then wiped dry or glazed off. *Glazed off* means to leave some of the color on top of the wood.

Oil colors are easy to use and easy to remove. They do not penetrate deeply into the wood. If you apply a coat of oil stain and decide you do not like the color, simply wash it off with paint or lacquer thinner and restain with another color.

These stains are mellow, semitransparent colors that lay on top of the wood rather than penetrate deeply into it. The stain will slightly bleed into finishes that are applied over them. They are not light fast and will fade if exposed to the sun for a lengthy time. They do not raise the grain, so sanding is not necessary. Oil colors dry rapidly, in about 30 minutes.

Oil stains are available in concentrated form without thinner and in ready mix cans with thinner added.

### Concentrated oil colors

Concentrated oil colors are thick, heavy stains such as:

- Artists linseed oil, in tubes
- Linseed oil colors (color in oil)
- Universal colorant

These concentrated colors must be mixed with paint thinner before they can be used. They may also be thinned with turpentine, benzol, or lacquer thinner. Universal colorant is also soluble in water.

These versatile stains can be mixed with lacquer and varnish to make colors. They can be glazed over bare wood and finishes, or they can be mixed with lacquer and sprayed on wood or over finishes.

Universal colorant also can be used to color latex paint. I prefer to make my own stain using concentrated oil colors. They are similar to premixed colors, except I add the thinner. You can mix oil colors to make any shade you want and in any quantity you need. For small projects, blend the colors on a mixing board or a smooth hard surface, thin it with paint thinner, and apply it with a rag. To change the color, simply mix in other oil colors. For large projects, mix the stain with paint thinner in a large container; a coffee can works well.

### Premixed oil colors

Premixed colors usually come in pint and quart cans. After stirring, they can be applied directly from the container without thinning, for the thinner has already been added by the paint manufacturer.

A problem with premixed oil colors is finding the proper shade. You might need to buy more than one can of stain to find a color that is right. Each manufacturer makes several different colors, each with their own special names. For example: walnut, light walnut, dark walnut, antique walnut, danish walnut, and on and on. The colors vary between manufacturers. Walnut color from one manufacturer will not be the same color as walnut from another manufacturer.

To help the consumer select the proper stains, paint stores often display wood samples colored with their stains. If the wood in the sample is the same wood as your project, you know how the stain will look on the piece. If it is not the same wood, the color will probably be different. If the same walnut stain is applied to different woods, like walnut, maple, or pine, each will look different. Woods vary in density and porosity. Each will absorb different amounts of stain, and none will match.

## OIL STAIN APPLICATION

Stains can be applied with a rag, a paintbrush, or by dipping or spraying. The usual method of application is with a rag. A cloth is dipped in stain and rubbed on the wood one section at a time. When the section is evenly covered, a clean rag is used to wipe off excess stain. A brush can be used to push stain into hard to reach grooves and corners or to brush an entire piece.

Small items can be dipped in stain. This works well with furniture pulls and knobs. Immerse the piece in a container of stain. When coated, pull it out and remove excess stain with a cloth.

Use a spray gun to spray stain on large cabinets and panels. Spraying speeds the application, gives a uniform coating, and darkens hard to stain grooves.

*Materials*

Concentrated or premixed oil colors

Rubber gloves or hand-protect cream

Soft cotton rags

Paint thinner

Paintbrush

Mixing board such as a sheet of glass, metal, or formica

To protect your hands, apply hand-protect cream. Rub it in, concentrating on the fingernails. Or wear rubber gloves.

### Applying concentrated oil color

Take a small amount of each of the stains that are going to be blended and place them on a mixing board or a smooth hard surface of glass, metal, or formica. Pour a small amount of paint thinner on the thick concentrated colors and blend them together with a rag (FIG. 7-2). Test the color by first staining a scrap of wood from the piece, or by staining an obscure part of the piece, such as a back, lower rear side, or inside leg.

If the color is right, continue staining, adding more color and paint thinner as needed. Keep the stain rag wet with stain and thinner so the color can flow out and evenly coat the piece. If you wish to make minor changes in the stain, add new colors until the desired shade is obtained.

On large cabinets or projects with several pieces that cannot all be stained at the same time, mix enough stain to cover the entire project. Mix color in a wide mouth jar or coffee can and seal it for future use. On large projects, it might be easier to buy premixed oil colors that come in quart cans.

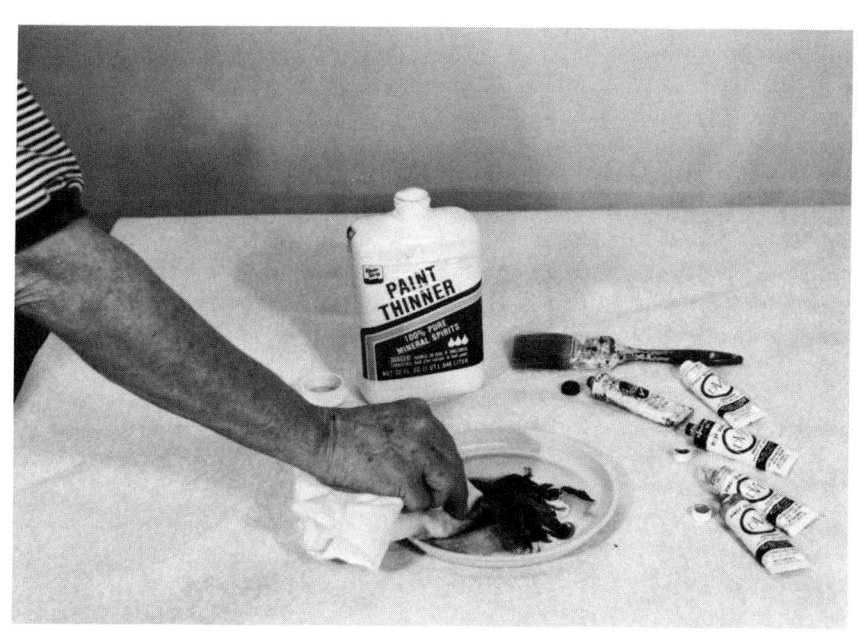

**7-2** Blending concentrated oil colors.

Apply the stain with a soft cotton rag; old cotton diapers are excellent (FIG. 7-3). Continue adding color and paint thinner to the mixing board, blending the colors and soaking them into the rag. Wipe the stain onto the wood following the grain. Force stain into grooves and crevices. Use a paintbrush dipped in stain to color hard to reach spots.

When the project is evenly colored, before it dries, wipe off excess stain with a clean cloth, following the grain (FIG. 7-4). Wiping lightly leaves more stain on the wood and gives a darker color; wiping hard removes more stain and gives a lighter color. When the piece is too light, a second application of stain might darken it further. If too dark, washing the wood with paint thinner will remove more color. If the color is still too dark, wash the wood with lacquer thinner, which will remove most of the stain from hard woods.

Determine the color of the wood while it is wet with stain. This is also the time to tell how the stain will look when a finish is applied over it. As stain dries, it looks dull and dead, and does not give a true indication of its color or how it will look when a finish is applied. Do not be disappointed or restain the piece. When a finish is applied, the color will come to life, and the true color of the stained wood will appear. Determine the color of the stain while it is wet on the wood, not after it dries.

Stain must be thoroughly dry before applying a finish. Oil stains dry from 30 to 60 minutes, depending on the temperature. Stain dries rapidly when hot, sometimes too fast. On warm days, if the stain dries too fast to properly wipe or glaze it off, add a retarder to the glaze to slow its drying time. The retarder can be purchased from finishing supply companies.

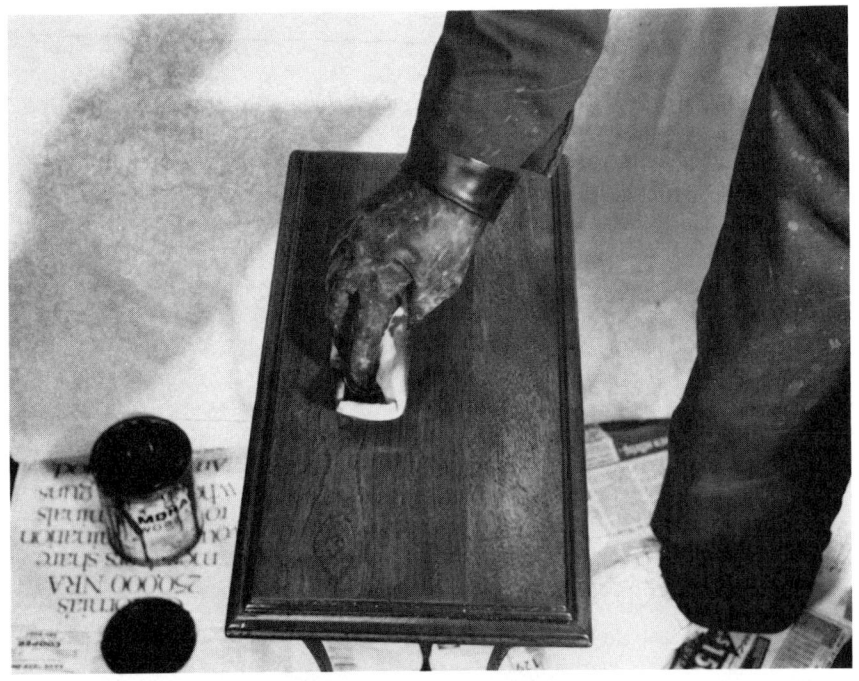

**7-3** Apply a wet, even coat of stain with a rag or brush.

**7-4** Wipe off excess stain with a soft cloth.

Stain is dry and ready to be finished over when it turns completely dull, with no shiny wet spots anywhere—not in the pores, corners, or grooves. If a finish is applied over wet stain, especially a lacquer finish, it will turn white. Correct this problem by allowing the finish to dry; then recoating it with a wet finish coat.

## Applying premix oil colors

In relation to application, everything that was said about applying concentrated oil colors is true of premixed colors. They are applied, wiped, and dried in the same way. The difference is, colors are not blended nor is paint thinner added to the premixed colors. The heavy concentrated colors used to make premixed stains settle to the bottom of the container, and they must be frequently stirred while being used. If a lighter stain is needed, do not stir. Use the lighter stain at the top of the can. For a darker stain, scrape some of the heavy pigment from the bottom of the can and use it.

*Materials*

Premixed oil colors

Paint thinner

Paintbrush and rags

Rubber gloves or hand-protect cream

*Application*

1. Remove finish and sand wood.
2. Apply premixed colors directly from the container after a thorough stirring.
3. Test the stain on an obscure part.
4. Apply stain with a rag, brush, or both.
5. Wipe off excess stain with a soft cloth.
6. Add second or third coats to darken.
7. Judge the color of the stain while it is wet.

## Highlighting

To add highlights when staining, do not wipe all of the stain out of grooves and carvings on turnings and decorations. Leave a little darker color behind to add contrasting highlights.

## Picture framing

To obtain a pleasing picture frame effect when staining tops, leave more color around the edges of the top. When stain has been applied to the top and is being glazed out, rub a little harder in the center of the top to remove more color and lighten the center.

## Uniforming

On tabletops and other furniture parts, the old cabinet makers often glued several boards together to make one large piece. When finish and stain is removed from these pieces, you'll find that the boards used to make the piece are not all the same color; some are light, some are dark. To uniform the color of the boards, it is necessary to carefully stain the lighter boards to match the adjoining dark wood. This is called *uniforming* or, as the old finishers called it, *sap staining*.

Often chairs are made with two or more different woods. Again the lighter wood parts in the chair should be stained to match the darker parts.

It is easy to darken light parts, but difficult to lighten the dark pieces.

## Self-sealing stains

Sealing stains have resin and color added to them. When applied to wood, they harden in the wood, sealing and staining at the same time. When dry, the color will not rub off. To make your own, add a small amount of varnish or penetrating sealer to oil stain.

## Varnish stains

Do not use colored varnish. This product finishes and stains at the same time. Avoid this one, for when applied, it muddies and obscures the wood. It is difficult to apply without uneven, muddy-colored brush streaks.

## WOODS AND STAIN

Walnut is rich in color and does not always need staining, especially dark walnut and antique walnut that has darkened with age. Burnt umber is a good stain to color walnut.

Mahogany is a beautiful wood that can be left natural or stained brown or red. Burnt umber works well with mahogany.

Oak and ash can be colored in many ways—two-tone with a black background and white in the pores; limed oak, with white thinly glazed across the wood finish; golden oak. These finishes have gone out of style and have been replaced with modern light brown and walnut colors. Burnt umber and walnut stains work well with oak and ash.

Maple and birch are hard, close-grained woods that can be stained with raw sienna for a yellow maple; burnt sienna for red maple; or burnt umber for a pleasing brown color.

Cherry is a fine, hard, cabinet wood that is beautiful when finished natural. A pleasing brown color can be obtained by using burnt umber.

Gum and poplar are soft woods that can be stained to look like walnut or mahogany. They are often stained to match these more expensive woods.

Pine is light colored, closed grain, and soft. Apply stain sparingly because this soft wood can absorb too much stain, causing the wood to become dark and muddy. It is an excellent wood to paint. A thin coat of sealer applied before staining will restrict the stain's penetration, giving a lighter color.

Fir has alternating streaks of soft and hard grain. Because of this grain difference, it is difficult to evenly stain. The hard grain absorbs little color; while the soft grain absorbs more color and darkens. To remedy this light and dark effect, apply a thin wash coat of sealer prior to staining, 50 percent thinner to 50 percent sealer. When the sealer dries, rub stain over the sealer and glaze it off with a soft cloth.

### Basic furniture colors

Pigmented oil colors such as burnt umber makes brown mahogany and walnut; raw umber makes brown walnut; burnt sienna makes red maple, when mixed with burnt umber gives cherry and mahogany; raw sienna makes maple yellow. These colors can be used individually or mixed together to make most furniture colors.

My favorite concentrated oil color is burnt umber. It looks good on all woods. It is best on walnut and mahogany, but gives the other woods a beautiful old brown cast. Other useful oil colors are Vandyke brown; lamp black; flake white; drop white; yellow ocher; chrome yellow, light, medium and dark; chrome green, light and dark; bulletin red; toluidine red; rose lake; and ultramarine blue.

## GLAZING

*Glazing* is applying a thin coat of color over bare wood or finish. The finish can be lacquer, varnish, urethane, or a painted surface. Glazing over a painted surface is called *antiquing*. The glaze color can be any of the colors in oil (see oil colors) or any colored paint or enamel that is thinned with mineral spirits (paint thinner).

Unlike staining, which is putting color in the wood, glazing is laying a thin coat of color on top of wood; applying color across the surface to give fine parallel lines following the grain. Glazing adds color to the wood and can give a grain pattern when none exists. Color is being glazed on a wood top in FIG. 7-5. Glazing works well on pine, maple, birch, gum, beech, and painted surfaces.

When dark and light woods are used together, their colors can be uniformed, or matched in color to the surrounding wood. Glazing gives the finish a mellowness by lightly obscuring the sharp details of the grain and giving depth to the finish. Glaze color left in grooves and corners gives the appearance of age, imitating an antique. Glaze can be used to darken or change the color of a finish; maple can be made to look like walnut or mahogany.

### Glaze application

The glaze colors—concentrated oil colors, premixed oil colors, or oil-base paints—are thinned with paint thinner. When glazing over varnish or

**7-5** Glaze color over bare wood or an existing finish.

urethane, add a small amount of varnish or urethane to the color and paint thinner. Adding varnish will harden the glaze, assuring that the glaze will not be disturbed when the clear protective finish is later applied. If the glaze color is an oil paint, adding varnish is not necessary because resin in the paint will harden the glaze.

To glaze over lacquer, use oil colors and paint thinner only. Do not add varnish or use oil-base paint as a glaze color. They are not compatible with lacquer. An oil color thinned with paint thinner could easily be rubbed or brushed off. There is no resin added to make it adhere to the surface. Because lacquer is sprayed, the glaze will not be disturbed when the finish is sprayed over the glazed surface. If the glaze is accidentally rubbed off prior to finishing, it must be reapplied.

Mix the glaze in a shallow pan:

1. For use over a varnish finish—4 tablespoons paint thinner, 1 teaspoon color, and 1 tablespoon varnish.
2. For use over a urethane finish—4 tablespoons paint thinner, 1 teaspoon color, and 1 tablespoon urethane.
3. For use over lacquer—4 tablespoons paint thinner and 1 teaspoon color.

If the glaze is too thick, add more paint thinner. If the color is too light, add more color. Changing the consistency of the glaze will vary the grain pattern.

Apply the glaze to the surface with a soft cotton rag folded to form a smooth pad without any wrinkles, seams, or button holes on its bottom. Dip the rag into the glaze color and spread it evenly across the finish.

Before the color dries, carefully wipe it off with the grain. Wipe from one side to the other without lifting the glazing rag from the surface. Leave the edges of tops just a little darker by removing more color from the center of the top.

Color left behind can simulate grain and give highlights and shadows. Glaze left in flutes, carvings, and moldings will add accents. Ideally, grain lines should be fine, light, equidistant lines running with the grain. Avoid heavy, harsh, uneven graining.

The size of the glaze lines will depend on the thickness of the glaze, the coarseness of the rag, and the pressure used on the glazing pad. A thinner glaze color flows out leaving light grain lines; a thick glaze gives heavy, dark glaze lines. A smooth soft glaze rag gives fine grain lines; a coarse glazing rag gives coarse, heavy lines.

A soft glazing brush can be used in place of a rag. It makes it easy to get into corners without leaving blotches.

Variation in the grain pattern can be obtained by using different graining materials and techniques. Light pressure on the glaze rag will leave a heavy glaze on the surface. Heavy pressure removes most of the glaze leaving a light glaze behind. Use coarse steel wool or burlap for a rough-textured grain pattern. If the glaze is not right, clean it off with paint thinner and try again. Experiment; it is fun. Let the glaze dry overnight for varnish and urethane, or 1 hour for lacquer. Apply a final coat of clear finish for protection.

Although any color can be used to make glazes, burnt umber, raw umber, raw sienna, and black are frequently used. To use gold as a glaze, add 1 teaspoon of linseed oil to the glaze mixture. Linseed oil helps the gold to flow out smoothly and evenly.

Slow-drying glazing liquids can be purchased from finishing supply dealers. Glazing liquids dry slowly, giving more time to work with the glaze before it dries.

## ANTIQUING

There are three steps to follow when antiquing. First, the wood is painted with an opaque paint or enamel called the *base coat*. Often used colors are off-white or ivory, red, blue, green, or any base color you like. Second, to give highlights or a grain pattern, a thin transparent glaze color is rubbed over the dried base coat and partially wiped off. Raw umber color is frequently used; burnt umber, black, raw sienna and gold can also be used. Finally, to protect the glaze, a final coat of clear finish can be applied.

Although any wood can be antiqued, stop and think. Do you really want to paint over a fine antique or wood like walnut, mahogany, cherry, oak, or teak? These pieces should be coated with a clear finish to preserve their value or to bring out their beauty. It is best to antique furniture that is made with inexpensive wood such as pine, fir, gum or poplar.

The base coat can be applied to bare or finished wood. If the finish on the piece being antiqued is intact and is not peeling or cracking, then all that is needed to prepare the surface is to clean and sand it.

If hardware (knobs, pulls, metal trim) can be easily removed, take them off. Clean the finish with water and a mild detergent; dry thoroughly. Clean again with a rag that is saturated with paint thinner. Next, sand the finish with 180-grit sandpaper. Small dents and scratches will give it an antique look.

When antiquing over unfinished "bare" wood that is porous (oak, ash, mahogany, walnut, or teak), a good practice is to first apply one coat of clear on the surface sealer over the wood. The purpose is to keep colored enamel out of pores, grooves, and cracks. Later, if you want to refinish the piece to a natural finish, paint remover will easily clean off the color. When enameling over porous wood without a clear sealer, the colored enamel will be almost impossible to remove from pores.

After the wood or finish has been prepared, apply one or two coats of satin or semigloss colored enamel (FIG. 7-6). Apply two coats for unfinished wood, one coat for a finished surface; if the surface is rough or not evenly coated, apply a second coat. When spraying lacquer, use two coats. To antique small projects, and if the right color can be found, an aerosol spray will make applying the finish easier. Sand between coats with 400-grit sandpaper and water.

To glaze, rub glaze color evenly over the enamel, forcing it into every crack and corner. Before it dries, wipe it off evenly with the grain (FIG. 7-7). Leave some color behind on the surface and in grooves and cracks

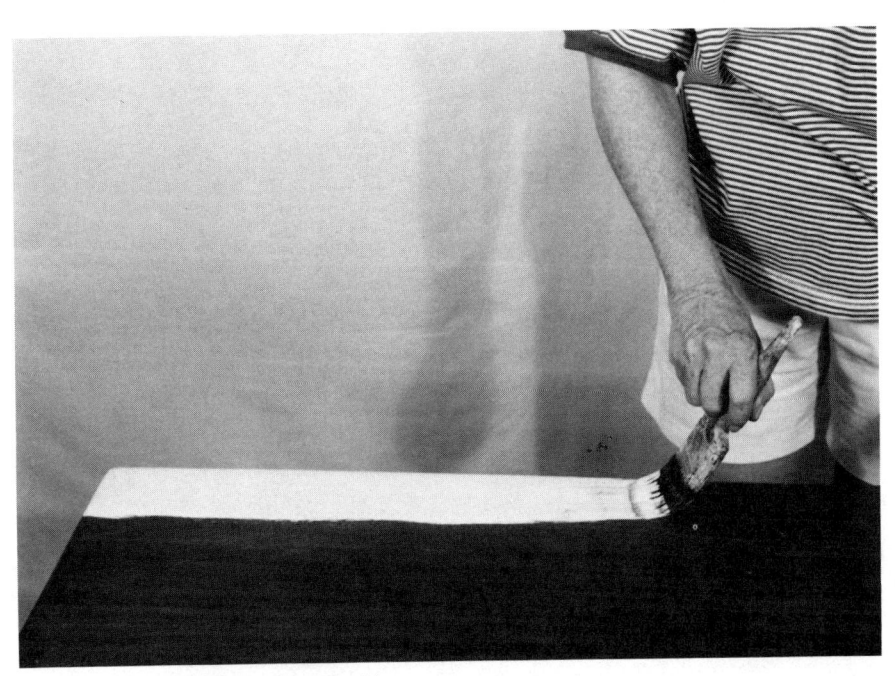

**7-6** Coat the surface with a colored base coat.

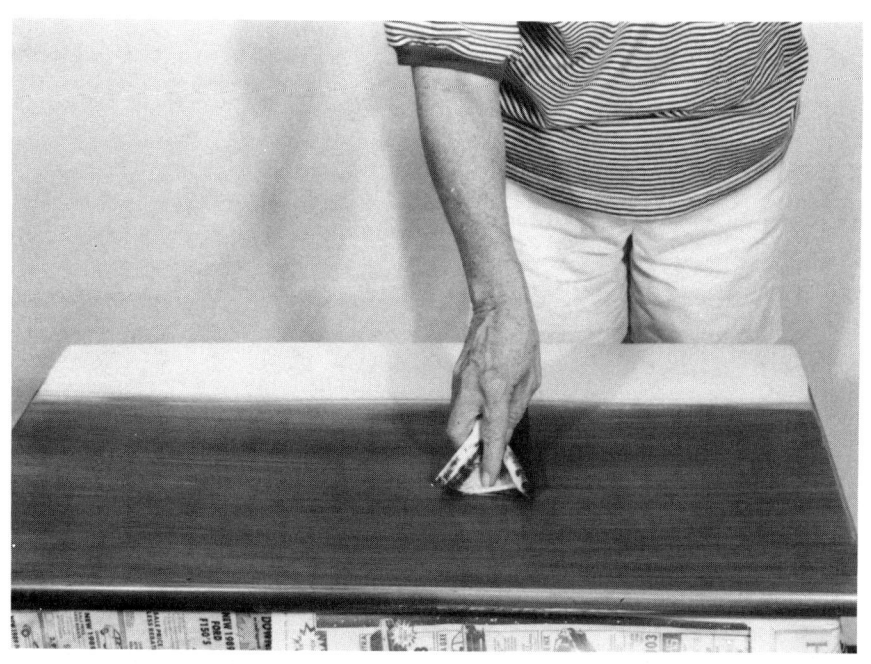

**7-7** Glaze color over the painted surface.

**7-8** Apply a clear, protective finish over the dried glaze.

(see glaze mixing and application). If you are not satisfied with the glaze color or application, clean it off with paint thinner and try again.

After the glaze coat dries (turns dull), usually overnight, seal it with a clear protective finish. Clear satin or gloss varnish is applied when an enamel base color is used. Clear satin or gloss lacquer is used over a colored lacquer base. Figure 7-8 shows a finished glazed surface.

Antiquing kits that contain antiquing materials can be purchased from paint and hardware stores. The kit should contain a ready-mixed base color and a contrasting glazing liquid. Some also supply a protective finish, sandpaper, and steel wool.

*Materials*

Clear sealer, if bare wood is being antiqued

Opaque base color

Glaze color

Paint thinner

Mixing board of glass, metal, or plastic

Soft cotton rags

Soft-bristle brush

Clear protective finish

*Application*

1. Apply base color to wood or finish, allow to dry.
2. Rub glaze color onto the surface and lightly wipe off with the grain.
3. When the glaze color dries, apply a protective coat of clear finish.

# Chapter 8
# Pore filling

*To* get a smooth glass-like surface on open-pored wood, it might be necessary to fill the cell cavities (pores) with pore filler. Pores can be filled with sanding sealer, but this method takes considerable time. A better method is to use heavy-bodied paste pore filler. This inexpensive filler is rubbed into the pores to fill them quickly. Good commercially prepared pore fillers contain silex, which is a finely ground quartz, and a dryer, linseed oil, and thinner.

Woods with open pores are candidates for pore filler: oak, ash, hickory, mahogany, and chestnut. Woods that have small pores or no pores do not need filling: maple, birch, pine, cedar, redwood, and cherry. Sanding sealer will fill the pores on these close-grained woods.

Using pore filler is an optional step. Many finishers like their finishes to have a natural open-pored look. Wood that is being finished with an in-the-wood finish (linseed oil, tung oil, and penetrating resin sealers) is not filled.

Pore filler is available in clear or with walnut and mahogany colors added. Colored fillers will stain and fill at the same time. Oil colors can be added to the natural filler to match the color of stained wood. Colored filler lightens when dry, so color it slightly darker. Darkening the pores can give a pleasing contrast to the lighter surrounding wood.

Paste filler is thick and heavy in the container. Before it can be rubbed into the pores, it must be stirred until it has a creamy consistency.

## PASTE PORE FILLER APPLICATION

Apply paste filler to a porous wood surface that has been sanded smooth, stained if desired, and sealed with a thin coat of sanding sealer. Thin paste filler with paint thinner and thoroughly stir it to a creamy consistency. Because filler quickly settles to the bottom of the container, stir it often.

**8-1** Brush on pore filler with the grain.

Brush the filler onto the wood with a stiff, short-bristled brush. Work the filler into the pores by brushing it lengthwise with the grain. Force it into the pores. The cell cavities must be completely filled (FIG. 8-1).

When the filler begins to dull, from 10 to 20 minutes, wipe off excess filler with a coarse cloth; burlap is good. Rub briskly across the grain, removing excess filler from the surface of the wood (FIG. 8-2). Do not rub with the grain at this time or you will pull some of the soft filler out of the pores. If the filler is allowed to dry too hard before it is cleaned off, it will

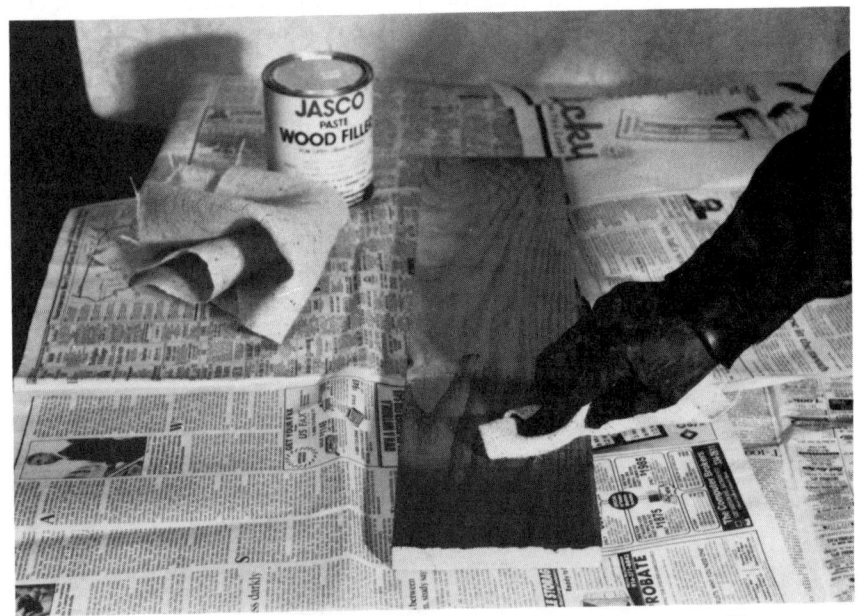

**8-2** Wipe cross-grain with a coarse cloth (burlap is good) to remove excess filler.

be difficult to remove. To finish the filler removal, lightly rub the wood with a clean cloth in the direction of the grain, removing cross lines of filler left by the first cross-grain rubbing. Rub lightly to prevent filler from being pulled from the pores.

When the surface is cleaned, allow the wood to dry overnight at 70 degrees or higher. When dry, lightly sand with 280-grit sandpaper. Sand with the grain to remove any filler that might still be on the wood (FIG. 8-3). Unwanted filler left on the surface will appear as streaks when a finish is applied.

**8-3** Lightly sand to remove dried filler from the surface.

The final step is to seal the surface with sanding sealer. Continue with the finish application.

Pore fillers that contain silex and linseed oil are used with varnish finishes. This type of filler will also work with lacquer, but it must be thoroughly dry before coating with lacquer, at least 24 hours. If you use a lacquer finish, try to find a pore filler made to be used with lacquer. It should not contain linseed oil: read the label.

*Materials*

Paste pore filler, colored or natural

Oil colors

Paint thinner

Stiff-bristle brush

Coarse rags, burlap

280-grit sandpaper

Sanding sealer

*Application*

1. Remove finish and sand the wood.
2. Stain (optional).
3. Seal the wood (50 percent thinner to 50 percent sanding sealer).
4. Apply the filler with a stiff brush. Push it into the grain, then smooth it out with the grain.
5. When the filler dulls (from 5 to 15 minutes), rub it across the grain with a coarse rag to remove excess filler from the wood.
6. Finish the filler removal by lightly rubbing with the grain.
7. Dry overnight.
8. Lightly sand with 280-grit sandpaper.
9. Apply sanding sealer and top coats.

# Chapter 9

# Applying finishes

*E*ach finish is unique and must be applied in its own special way. This chapter describes finishes and how to apply them step by step.

## SEALERS

Sealers help obtain a smooth, level surface on open-pored wood (oak, ash, and mahogany). One or two coats of sanding sealer is sprayed or brushed on the wood. Figure 9-1 shows commonly used sealers.

Sealers are first-coat finishes that are applied to the wood to keep pitch and stains from bleeding into top coats. They help fill pores and provide a smooth, level surface for top coats to lay on. When sealer has been applied and sanded, one or two top coats of satin or gloss finish is applied over the sealer.

### Varnish sealer

Applying varnish sanding sealer is an optional step, and its use is not mandatory. If you do use a sealer under varnish, use varnish sanding sealer.

### Urethane sealer

The use of a sealer under urethane is optional and not always needed. Closely follow the product's instruction. If you use a sealer, make sure it is made for use with a urethane finish.

### Lacquer sealer

When finishing with lacquer, always use lacquer sanding sealer when finishing bare or stained wood. Only use lacquer sanding sealer under a lacquer finish.

**9-1** First coat sealers (from left to right): urethane sealer, shellac, varnish sanding sealer, and lacquer sanding sealer.

Do not use lacquer under or over varnish or urethane. Lacquer applied over varnish will lift the varnish, literally bubbling and peeling it off the wood. Lacquer under urethane might cause the urethane to peel off.

## Shellac sealer

Shellac is excellent to seal pitch or stains that bleed out of wood, but it does not sand as easy as sanding sealer. Varnish or lacquer can safely be applied over shellac. Except to seal stains and resins in wood, it is best to use a modern varnish or lacquer sanding sealer.

## Oil and penetrating resin finishes

These thin penetrating finishes are sealers. They soak into the wood and harden. No special sealer is needed or should be used with them.

## Tack rag

A tack rag is a cheese cloth that has been impregnated with a sticky resin. When it is wiped across a surface or finish, it removes dirt and dust particles. Its use is a must when finishing with varnish or urethane.

Wiping a dry cloth across a surface does not remove dust or dirt. There is an electrical attraction between the dirt particles and the surface. Wiping only moves these dirt particles around and probably leaves lint from the rag behind as well. The bumps on varnish and urethane finishes that are called air bubbles are usually dust spots. Using a tack rag helps to eliminate many of these bumps.

When using the tack rag, lightly whisk it across the surface. Hard rubbing could leave resin from the cloth on the surface. If this resin is lacquered over, the lacquer finish might not dry.

## VARNISH FINISH APPLICATION

If you choose to use a sanding sealer when varnishing, brush one coat of varnish sealer on wood that has small pores, such as maple, birch, walnut, or cherry. Use two or more coats of sealer on wood with large pores, such as oak, ash, and mahogany; lightly sand between coats. Varnish sanding sealer does not need thinning. After thoroughly stirring, brush it on as it comes from the container.

*Materials*

Varnish sanding sealer
Varnish satin or gloss
Clean can
Clean 2-inch bristle brush
Paint thinner
Nylon stocking
Tack rag
400-grit wet or dry sandpaper
Water

*Application*

1. Sand the wood smooth and stain it.
2. Clean the surface with a tack rag.
3. Stir the sanding sealer and strain through a nylon stocking into a clean can.
4. Brush a heavy coat of sealer onto the wood.
5. Dry overnight. Sand with 400-grit sandpaper and water.
6. Clean the surface with a tack rag.
7. Strain satin or gloss varnish into a clean can and brush onto surface.
8. Dry for two days.
9. Sand the dried varnish surface with 400-grit sandpaper to remove dust spots. Use water as a lubricant.
10. Rub with steel wool or pumice stone. See Chapter 13, *Hand-Rubbed Finishes*.

## VARNISH FINISH APPLICATION WITHOUT A SEALER

If you do not use a sealer, the first coat of varnish can be used as a sealer. Thin the first varnish coat with 3 tablespoons of paint thinner to 1 cup of varnish. When brushed on the wood, the thinned finish can penetrate into the wood, allowing air trapped in pores to escape without leaving air bubbles in the finish.

After the first coat dries, lightly sand it with water and 400-grit wet or dry sandpaper. Wipe the sanded surface dry, then clean it with a tack cloth. Apply a final coat of varnish. Thin the second coat with 1 tablespoon of paint thinner to 1 cup of varnish. Although not always necessary, additional varnish coats can be applied.

The work area and varnish should be warm, about 70 degrees. Wear work clothes that are clean and dust free. Sprinkle the floor with water to hold down dust. Avoid drafts that could carry dust into the room.

To prepare varnish, use a clean, new, 2-inch bristle brush (hog bristle). Thoroughly stir, especially satin and flat finishes, then strain the varnish through a nylon stocking into a clean container (FIG. 9-2). For the first coat, add 3 tablespoons of paint thinner to 1 cup of varnish. For the second coat, add 1 tablespoon of paint thinner to 1 cup varnish.

**9-2** Strain the finish through a nylon stocking or paint strainer to remove lumps and dirt.

To prepare wood, clean the wood surface with a tack cloth. Lightly wipe the surface of the wood with the cloth to remove dust particles (FIG. 9-3).

To apply varnish, wet horizontal surfaces with a generous even amount of varnish. Brush the finish on following the grain, evenly coating the entire surface (FIG. 9-4). Next, brush cross-grain to evenly cover the surface (FIG. 9-5). Then, to smooth and level the finish, hold the brush at a

*Varnish finish application without a sealer* 81

**9-3** Remove dust from the surface with a tack cloth.

**9-4** Apply the finish with the grain, use a clean bristle brush.

**9-5** Brush cross-grain to thoroughly cover the surface.

45-degree angle with the tip of the brush lightly touching the surface. Draw it across the wet varnish. Begin at one end and finish at the other without raising the brush from the surface (FIG. 9-6). Move rapidly. Modern varnish finishes dry quickly.

**9-6** To smooth the finish, lightly draw the brush across the surface, following the grain.

Once the finish has been applied and brushed out (tipped off), leave it alone except to brush out runs on vertical surfaces. Overbrushing could cause brush lines if a modern, fast-drying varnish is used.

After the first coat of varnish dries, two days or more, lightly sand the finish with 400-grit wet or dry sandpaper and water. Use a sandpaper block on flat surfaces.

As the finish is sanded, dull spots will denote sanded off high spots on the finish, the tops of dust spots, and brush lines. Shiny areas are low spots that have not been sanded, the valleys of brush streaks, and pores. Ideally, a surface is smooth when there are no shiny spots, just a smooth, dull surface.

It is not possible to have a completely smooth, dull surface with one coat of finish; it might take several. If you sand through the finish, immediately stop sanding in that area and move on. You can restain the sanded-through spots using the original stain color, then revarnish it to cover the bare spots.

When the first varnish coat has been sanded, apply a second coat. This time use 1 tablespoon of paint thinner to 1 cup of varnish. Apply the second coat using the same methods as was used for applying the first. Clean the surface with a tack cloth. Apply a wet even coat, carefully tipping it off with the tip of the brush.

If the finish has been applied wet and evenly with no bare spots, two coats should be adequate. The finish can now be rubbed, or if you choose not to rub, use and enjoy!

*Materials*

Varnish, satin or gloss
Clean, 2-inch bristle brush

Clean can

Paint thinner

Nylon stocking

Tack rag

400-grit wet or dry sandpaper

*Application*

1. Sand the wood smooth and stain it.
2. Clean the surface with a tack rag.
3. Stir the varnish and strain through a nylon stocking into a clean can.
4. First coat: add 3 tablespoons paint thinner to 1 cup varnish; brush on the wood.
5. Dry for two days, then lightly sand with 400-grit sandpaper and water to remove dust spots.
6. Second coat: add 1 tablespoon of paint thinner to 1 cup varnish; brush on wood.
7. Dry for two days.
8. Sand with 400-grit sandpaper to remove dust spots. Rub with steel wool or pumice stone. See the chapter on rubbing finishes.

## URETHANE FINISHES

When applying urethane finishes, follow the instructions for varnish application, with this exception. Most urethane finishes cannot be applied over varnish or lacquer sanding sealer. Urethane does not adhere well to these sealers or finishes, and it might peel off. When a sealer is used under urethane, it must be made for a urethane finish. Urethane sealers are usually thin, watery, penetrating sealers. They can be applied with a brush or rag, allowed to soak in, then wiped dry.

Some urethanes cannot be applied over a stain that contains a stearate dryer. It is not always possible to tell if a stain contains a stearate dryer. As a precaution when using an oil stain, add a little urethane sealer to the color. It slows the stain's drying time but ensures that the urethane will not later peel.

Buy oil-thinnable urethane that is thinned with paint thinner. Do not use urethane that is hardened with a catalyst or thinned with water. Urethane is made to dry with either a gloss or satin sheen. It can be brushed or sprayed. Other urethane type finishes are varathane and polyurethane.

*Materials*

Sealer (optional)

Urethane, gloss or satin

Clean 2-inch bristle brush

Clean can

Nylon stocking

Tack rag

400-grit wet or dry sandpaper

Water

Spray equipment (optional)

*Application*

1. Sand the wood smooth and stain it.
2. Apply sealer to wood (optional).
3. Strain urethane finish through a nylon stocking into a clean can.
4. First coat: add 3 tablespoons of paint thinner to 1 cup of urethane; brush or spray onto wood.
5. Dry according to manufacturer's recommendation. Sand with 400-grit wet or dry sandpaper; use water as a lubricant.
6. Clean the surface with a tack rag.
7. Apply a second strained coat of urethane thinned with 1 tablespoon of paint thinner to 1 cup of urethane.
8. Dry overnight.
9. Sand with 600-grit paper and water; rub with steel wool or pumice stone. Refer to the chapter on rubbing finishes.

## PREVENTING AND CORRECTING RUNS

When brushing chair or table legs with turnings on them, you'll find that high spots on the rungs pull more finish from the brush as you draw it across the knobs. This excess finish flows to the low valleys of the rungs and drips. To avoid these drips, rather than draw the brush across the full length of the rung, brush each knob individually; then pick up any runs that appear with the tip of the brush. It will be necessary to go back and check often to see if runs are forming. This is true of any vertical surface that is being brushed or sprayed.

If you find a run, brush up from the bottom of the run with the tip of the brush, either removing the run with the tip of the brush or brushing it back into the finish. To avoid runs when brushing vertical surfaces, such as the sides of dressers, chests, doors or panels, begin brushing at the bottom of the panel and work up to the top.

If runs form when spraying, immediately wipe them off or back them into the surrounding finish. Use a paintbrush, a lint-free cloth, or your hand. Wipe the run up from the bottom. If the wiped area is rough after the run has been removed, sand the area and respray.

You must wait until a run dries hard all the way through before attempting to sand it off. If you sand before the finish hardens, pieces of the run can pull off, leaving deep holes in the finish. Runs can be difficult to remove. Runs are thick, but the finish on either side of it is thin. When you try to sand off the run, you will quickly sand away thin finish on either side of it and expose bare wood.

To remove a run, tightly wrap 400-grit sandpaper around a small sandpaper block and carefully sand the run. Do not allow the paper to touch the finish on either side of it.

Another way to remove a run is to scrape it off with a single-edge razor blade. Hold the blade at a right angle to the run and scrape it back and forth across the surface, scraping off the high spot until it is flush with the surrounding finish. Be careful not to touch the finish on either side of the run or you will remove the finish there. Lightly sand to blend the scraped area into the surrounding finish. If you sand through the finish while trying to remove a run, stain the bare spot and recoat with finish. Note that the run must be completely dry before attempting to remove it.

These procedures for removing runs in varnish and urethane work equally as well with runs that form after spraying clear lacquer or other clear finishes.

## MILK PAINT FINISH

If you would like to make an antique finish, try mixing your own. Mix powdered milk with hot water until it has the consistency of paint. Experiment; if the finish is too thick, add more water; if too thin, add more powdered milk. To color, add water-soluble colors, dry powder colors, universal colorant, or any color you can find that will mix with water. When the paint is mixed, strain it into a clean container through a paint strainer or nylon stocking.

Milk paint should be applied hot to clean, bare wood. Remove any finish first. Just before the finish is applied, wet the wood with water using a damp cloth or sponge. Two coats of paint must be applied. Brush on the first coat and allow it to dry overnight; then apply the second coat. When the second coat is dry, rub the finish with 3/0 steel wool to smooth and brighten the finish.

Milk paint dries dead flat. An oil finish rubbed over the paint will give it more gloss. Tung oil, boiled linseed oil or danish oil can be used. Brush shellac or varnish over milk paint to seal it, then rub it to a satin sheen.

To simulate an antique finish, rub off some of the milk paint from the edges and other high-wear surfaces. Distress the finish by denting the surface with a hammer, screwdriver, or chains. These dents are called antique marks. Dust the surface with rottenstone or raw umber dry powder and wipe it off, leaving a little color behind in the dents and grooves. The last step is to apply a thin coat of oil finish. Clean brushes and containers with water after use.

*Materials*

Powdered milk and hot water

Dry colors

Brush (synthetic bristle)

Can and nylon stocking

Steel wool

*Application*

1. Sand wood smooth.
2. Mix powdered milk with water and colors, then strain it into a clean can.
3. Dampen the wood with water and apply one coat of hot milk paint.
4. Dry overnight.
5. Apply a second coat of warm, strained milk paint.
6. Dry overnight.
7. Rub with 2/0 steel wool.
8. Antique (optional step, see distressing).

## SHELLAC FINISH

Shellac can be used as a sealer or a finish. It is best used as a sealer with a more durable finish coat applied over it. Varnish and lacquer are both finishes that can be used over shellac.

Shellac is excellent to seal unwanted stain or pitch that might be in the wood. It keeps them from seeping out of the wood into top coats. Often, when applying a light-colored paint over wood that was previously stained with a red aniline dye, the red will bleed into the new paint, discoloring it. Shellac will seal the red dye into the wood. It will also hold tar and pitch in the wood, allowing the board to be painted without the problem of having stain or pitch later oozing through the new finish.

Shellac originally comes in crystal form. The crystals are dissolved in denatured alcohol. If 4 pounds of shellac crystals are mixed with 1 gallon of alcohol, it is called a *4-lb. cut*; 5 pounds of shellac crystals mixed with 1 gallon of alcohol is called *5-lb. cut*; and so on. It is much easier to buy premixed shellac from your hardware store—no mixing or mess. The crystals are dark and, when dissolved, have an amber color that is pleasing on dark wood, but not if you want a clear finish. The paint manufacturer bleaches the shellac to remove its dark color. Once opened, premix shellac has a short shelf life (about six months). Try to buy only what you need for your project.

*Materials*

Shellac, 1-lb. cut

Denatured alcohol

Wide-mouth jar

2-inch bristle brush

Rubbing oil or cream polish

280-grit sandpaper

4/0 steel wool

Spray equipment (optional)

Wax

*Application*

1. Sand wood smooth and stain it.
2. Brush or spray one coat of 1-lb. cut shellac.
3. Dry for 2 hours, then sand with 280-grit sandpaper.
4. Apply a second and third coat. Follow the instructions for applying the first coat.
5. Let the last coat dry for 24 hours.
6. Rub the dried finish with 4/0 steel wool. Use rubbing oil or cream polish as a lubricant.

To apply shellac, begin with 1-lb. cut shellac. Pour the thinned shellac into a jar with a lid; keep it tightly closed when not being used. Use a 2-inch bristle brush. Apply a full wet coat of shellac, overlapping each stroke. Shellac dries rapidly. You must apply it fast and evenly. If a small spot is missed, do not go back and try to rebrush the spot. The shellac is already drying, and it will streak.

The first coat will dry tack free in about 15 minutes and can be lightly sanded with 280-grit sandpaper in 2 hours. A second and third coat should be applied like the first.

**Satin finish**

Let the final coat dry 24 hours before rubbing it. Use 4/0 steel wool wet with rubbing oil or cream polish.

**Gloss finish**

For a high-gloss surface, apply a fourth coat of 2-lb. or 3-lb. cut shellac. When this coat dries, in about three days, rub it with pumice stone and rubbing oil. Avoid sanding or rubbing with water; it could turn the finish white or cloudy. Polish a shellac finish with a hard paste wax to make it look attractive and to protect it from water and alcohol.

For extra protection on high-wear surfaces, apply a coat of varnish in place of the wax.

## FRENCH POLISH FINISH

Early French finishers developed a unique finishing process called *French polishing*. The process is slow and time-consuming, but produces an appearance of depth and transparency not obtained by other finishing methods. This method can be used to repair damaged finishes or to produce a new finish. Slowly, several thin coats of shellac are rubbed on the wood with a cloth pad. The pad has a core of cotton wrapped with an outer cotton or linen cloth.

French polishing produces a beautiful finish, but because this method of finishing is time-consuming, it is not used commercially. Only the strong at heart should attempt it and only after practicing on a scrap or unwanted piece.

The wood must be sanded smooth with no burrs sticking up from the pores. Lightly dampening the wood prior to the last sanding will raise the burrs so they can be cut off with sandpaper. If the wood is to be stained, use a water aniline stain.

The rubbing pad is called a *rubber*. The center of the pad is composed of cotton or wool, about the size and shape of an egg. This core is wrapped with a linen or cotton outer cloth. The pad is shaped like a pear, pointed at one end and wide at the other.

If you are making your own shellacs from shellac crystals and denatured alcohol, use a thin, 1-lb. cut; though it is easier to buy commercially prepared white shellac. Do not shake or stir it.

Dip the cotton core of the pad into the shellac at the top of the can; it is lighter and thinner there. Squeeze the pad out. Wrap the outer cloth around the cotton ball. Add a little denatured alcohol to the outer pad and three or four drops of boiled linseed oil or oil of citronella. Whisk the pad across the surface making nonstop circles and figure eights with the pad until the surface is covered with a thin coating of shellac. Allow this finish to dry overnight.

Repeat the process until the finish is built up and has a high gloss. Add shellac and alcohol to the pad as needed. Use the oil sparingly, only a few drops at a time, or you will have an oily surface and no shellac finish. To clean off excess oil, add more alcohol to the pad and rub the surface.

It is not necessary to fill the pores, but if you choose to fill them, sprinkle pumice stone on the wood surface before the first coat of finish is applied. As the shellac is rubbed on with the rubber, pumice on the wood will cut off small particles of wood, take on the color of the wood, and fill the pores.

Another way to speed the application of French polish is to apply water-thin coats of shellac and sand between coats with 400-grit sandpaper. Finish by applying the remaining finish using the rubber pad to rub on the final coats.

If this high-gloss finish is too glossy, dull it by rubbing the final coat with 4/0 steel wool or fine pumice stone mixed with rubbing oil.

A French polished surface is made of shellac. Because shellac is not water or alcohol proof, apply paste wax over the finish to protect it from these hazards.

*Materials*

Shellac (white), 1-lb. cut

Denatured alcohol

Boiled linseed oil or citronella or olive oil

Rubbing pad (rubber)

Pumice

*Application*

1. Sand wood smooth and stain it with water-soluble aniline.

2. Sprinkle 4F pumice stone on the wood. Rub shellac on the surface with the rubber, forcing pumice into the pores.
3. Rub several thin coats of French polish on the wood with the rubber.
4. Apply oil, shellac, and alcohol as needed to the rubber and continue rubbing thin coats of shellac onto the wood until the surface is smooth and glossy.

## LINSEED OIL FINISH

To make a *traditional linseed oil finish*, mix:

1 tablespoon of siccative dryer,

1 pint boiled linseed oil, and

1/4 pint paint thinner.

Heat this mixture in a double boiler. (Be careful not to start a fire.) When the oil is warm, brush or rub it on the wood with a paintbrush or rag. If you like, you may use your hands to rub it into the wood. When the wood absorbs as much oil as it can, wipe the piece dry with a clean rag. Any oil left on the surface will become gummy. Repeat this process every day for one week; then once a month for six months. It takes considerable time and effort to apply this finish, but it is worth the effort when you see the beautiful finish this oil can produce.

To make a *modern linseed oil finish*, mix:

1 pint linseed oil;

1/2 pint varnish; and

1/2 pint paint thinner.

Heat and apply this mixture in the same way that was described for the traditional mixture, except three applications should be sufficient. This mixture is easier to apply, dries harder, and will not gum. These oil finishes can be varnished over for a more durable surface.

*Materials*

Oil colors

Boiled linseed oil, dryer, and paint thinner (varnish is optional)

Double boiler

Paintbrush or rags

*Application*

1. Sand wood and apply oil stain (optional).
2. Heat linseed oil mixture in a double boiler.
3. Apply heated oil to wood, allow it to soak in, then wipe dry.
4. Apply this mixture each day for one week; then once a month for six months.
5. Thoroughly wipe the oil from the wood after each application.

## TUNG OIL FINISH

Tung oil is an easy-to-apply transparent finish that is resistant to water, acid, alkali, and mildew. Before it is applied, the wood surface must be free of finish and sanded smooth. If a stain is used, it should be an oil stain.

Begin by pouring a small amount of polymerized tung oil into a shallow pan. Apply the oil with a brush or rag. Rub the oil into the wood with a soft cloth or your hands. Heat from your hands helps the oil penetrate into the wood. When the wood is saturated, rub off excess oil with a rag. If the oil becomes tacky, wipe it off with a cloth moistened in fresh tung oil. Allow the oil to dry overnight at room temperature.

Next, lightly buff the surface with 3/0 or 4/0 steel wool; then apply a second coat as you did the first. Repeat the process until you have obtained the proper luster. Three coats should be sufficient. For a hand-rubbed finish, rub the final coat with 4/0 steel wool.

Clean brushes and spills with paint or lacquer thinner. If small oil beads appear on the surface, rub them off with 4/0 steel wool that has been dipped in tung oil.

Buy small quantities of oil. Once opened, the oil begins to jell in the can. To keep air out, drop clean rocks or marbles into the container to displace air; then tighten the lid securely.

Rags used to apply tung oil can burn by spontaneous combustion. Soak them in water and discard them in a metal container.

*Materials*

Tung oil

Shallow pan

Soft cloth or paintbrush

Steel wool

*Application*

1. Sand wood and apply oil stain (optional).
2. Apply oil with a rag or paintbrush. Rub it in with a rag or your hands.
3. Thoroughly rub off excess oil; dry overnight.
4. Light buff the surface with 3/0 steel wool.
5. Apply a second and third coat of oil as was previously applied. Dry overnight between coats.
6. Rub the final coat with 4/0 steel wool.

## PENETRATING OIL FINISH

Penetrating sealers are simple to apply. The wood being finished must be free of old finish and must be sanded smooth. If the wood is to be stained, apply an oil stain. Manufacturers of penetrating sealers also make stains. If one is available, use it.

To finish, flood the surface with penetrating resin using a brush, rag, or your hands to rub it in. Allow the oil to soak in for 30 minutes on hardwood or 15 minutes for veneered surfaces. When the wood will absorb no more oil, thoroughly wipe away any remaining oil; set aside to dry overnight. Repeat this process until three coats are applied. After the final coat has dried for 24 hours, rub the finish with 3/0 or 4/0 steel wool.

Penetrating sealers dry flat but can be brightened by waxing or varnishing over for more gloss and durability.

*Materials*

Penetrating resin sealer

Shallow pan

Soft cloth or paintbrush

3/0 or 4/0 steel wool

*Application*

1. Sand wood smooth.
2. Apply stain with a rag or brush (optional).
3. Coat with penetrating sealer. Allow it to soak in about 30 minutes, then thoroughly rub off all remaining oil.
4. Dry overnight.
5. Repeat this process until three coats are applied.
6. Allow the final coat to dry for 24 hours.
7. When dry, rub with 3/0 or 4/0 steel wool.

## Penetrating sealer and urethane

To make a more durable penetrating sealer, one that is alcohol and water resistant, mix one part penetrating sealer and one part urethane. Apply one coat of penetrating sealer; then apply three to five coats of the oil and urethane mixture until the desired gloss is obtained.

*Materials*

Penetrating resin sealer and urethane finish

Soft rags

4/0 steel wool

*Application*

1. Sand the wood and apply an oil stain (optional).
2. For the first coat, apply straight penetrating sealer.
3. Dry for 24 hours.
4. Apply 50 percent penetrating sealer and 50 percent urethane mixture to wood.
5. Soak in for 15 minutes and wipe dry, then dry for 24 hours.

6. Apply 3 to 5 coats, until the proper sheen is obtained. Dry 24 hours between coats.
7. Rub the final coat with 4/0 steel wool.

## GILDING

Using gilding for ornamenting furniture and art objects with silver or gold dates back to the early Egyptians. The modern method of gilding is to brush on a mixture of *gold bronzing powder* mixed with varnish or lacquer.

You can get a smoother, brighter color by coating the surface with sticky sizing, varnish, or slow-drying lacquer. Sprinkle or rub dry bronzing powder into the tacky finish, then polish.

*Wax gilding* is another method that is easier to use than bronzing powder. Gold flakes are mixed with soft wax. When applied and buffed out, it resembles gold leaf.

## GOLD LEAF

*Gold leaf*, of course, is the finest gilding. Genuine gold leaf is expensive. Gold leaf is prepared by hammering gold into thin sheets 1/4000 inch thick. Gold leaf comes in books with twenty-five 4- or 5-inch sheets. The sheets of gold in the book are separated by thin tissues. These thin gold sheets are carefully laid over a smooth surface that has been coated with sizing, smoothed out, then coated with finish.

A less-expensive metal leaf can be used in place of gold or silver leaf with excellent results. Metal leaf can be applied to wood, plaster (Gesso), glass, or painted surfaces. The surface must be smooth and sealed.

Gold leaf is thin and will not cover wood grain or indentations. Lacquer or varnish sanding sealer can be used to seal bare wood. Plaster (Gesso) can also be used. This sealed surface is coated with slow-drying lacquer or varnish sizing. The sizing can be brushed or sprayed. When the size becomes tacky and will not stick to a finger, the metal leaf can be applied.

Carefully pick up a sheet of gold leaf and lay it on the sized surface. Avoid drafts; the slightest breeze will blow the thin sheets away. Pick the sheets up with your fingers or with a special gilder's brush. Rub the brush or fingers through your hair to pick up static electricity, which acts as a magnet to pick up the metal leaf. If pieces of the leaf break off, simply apply another. Overlap each leaf 1/4 inch, gently tapping it down with a cotton ball. If necessary, cut the sheets with sharp scissors. Smooth the leaf and burnish with a flannel or velvet pad. After 24 hours, to protect the leaf, apply a thin, clear coat of varnish or lacquer with a spray gun or aerosol.

*Materials*

Sizing

Gold or metal leaf

Gilder's brush (optional)
Scissors
Cotton ball
Flannel or velvet pad
Clear finish, varnish or lacquer

*Application*

1. Sand the surface smooth, seal it and color it (optional).
2. Apply sizing.
3. Lay gold leaf on the sizing and tap it down with a cotton ball.
4. Smooth the sheets with a flannel or velvet pad.
5. After 24 hours, apply a protective finish coating. Use a spray or aerosol.

# Chapter 10

# Lacquer finishing

*E*arlier, when I outlined the finishes, I said that lacquer was the easiest finish to apply and that it was the fastest-drying finish. Because lacquer dries quickly, it must be sprayed. To spray lacquer, you need special equipment—an air compressor to provide a continuous supply of air; a spray gun to apply the finish; and a spray area that is ventilated, clean, and well-lighted.

## LACQUER FINISHING EQUIPMENT

*Air compressors* compress air and deliver a continuous supply of air to the spray gun. Some compressors deliver air directly to the spray gun and run continuously; others store air in a tank, allowing the compressor motor to turn off when the tank is full. There are many small hand-held one-piece units that have the compressor and spray gun built into one piece. They can be used to spray fences but are not adequate to apply a fine lacquer finish.

An *air regulator* is attached to the air line between the air compressor and spray gun. It regulates air that goes from the compressor to the spray gun. About 35 to 45 pounds of air pressure are required to spray lacquer. Different paints require different air pressures. Heavy, thick paints require high air pressures; thin materials use low air pressures. You can adjust air regulators to deliver from 1 to 300 pounds of air. Turn the air regulator to the off position when not in use to relieve pressure on the regulator diaphragm.

*Condensers* are attached to commercial air regulators. The condenser removes water, oil, and dirt from the air, assuring a clean supply of air to the spray gun. The drain plug on the bottom of the condenser must be opened regularly to drain off moisture collected by the condenser. When attaching a condenser, mount it as far away from the air compressor as possible. This distance allows moisture in the air line to cool and condense before reaching the condenser.

A *spray booth* or spray area is an enclosure where fumes and spray dust are confined and exhausted outside the building. It is usually made of metal, with filters or a waterfall to clean the air. These booths are used in factories and finishing shops.

Spray booths do an excellent job of removing spray dust, but they are much too expensive to be installed in a home workshop. When spraying at home, place a fan by a doorway or open window in the spray area. There should be cross-ventilation to carry away fumes. Hang a tarp to confine spray dust. Keep the spray area clean; sweep the floors and walls or blow them clean. Clean spray booth filters or replace them regularly. The spray area needs to be well lighted. You must see the finish flowing onto the projects, top, sides, and insides. Side lighting is often necessary. Do not spray where spray dust or fumes could come in contact with flames, sparks, smoking, or gas water heaters or appliances. Fumes from lacquer and oil-base finishes are explosive.

A *turntable* is a stand that has a top much like a lazy Susan. The project being sprayed is placed on the top and rotated. You stand in one place and turn the table as you spray.

## SPRAY GUNS

There are several types of spray guns: internal mix, external mix, suction, and pressure. Each is made to be used with a certain type of finish or air compressor.

It is important that the spray gun be matched to the finish being sprayed and to the air compressor. The air compressor must produce a continuous supply of air to properly operate the spray gun. If a spray gun requires 6 cubic feet of air per minute to operate, the air compressor must put out at least 6 cubic feet of air per minute; if it doesn't, the gun will constantly be low on air, and the finish coming out of the spray gun will not be properly atomized.

*Vacuum-type external-mix spray guns* are used to spray lacquer. Air and lacquer is mixed (atomized) outside the spray gun, shaped, then blown out away from the gun onto the project (FIG. 10-1). They are excellent for spraying light-bodied finishes.

*Pressure-feed internal-mix spray guns* are used by painters to spray heavy-bodied paints. Air is forced into the material cup, pushing the finish up through the fluid tip where it is mixed with air inside the air cap (FIG. 10-2), then blown out of the gun onto the project. These guns use low air pressure and can be used with small, inexpensive air compressors.

*Bleeder spray guns* produce a continuous flow of air through them, even when the trigger on the spray gun is in the off position. This prevents a high air pressure buildup in the air lines and compressor. These guns are usually low quality and are used with small air compressors that do not have tanks to store air. They must run continuously.

*Nonbleeder spray guns* are equipped with an air valve that shuts off

**10-1** External mix air cap and fluid tip for spraying lacquer.

**EXTERNAL MIX**

**10-2** Internal mix air cap and fluid tip for spraying heavy-bodied finishes such as paint and enamels.

**INTERNAL MIX**

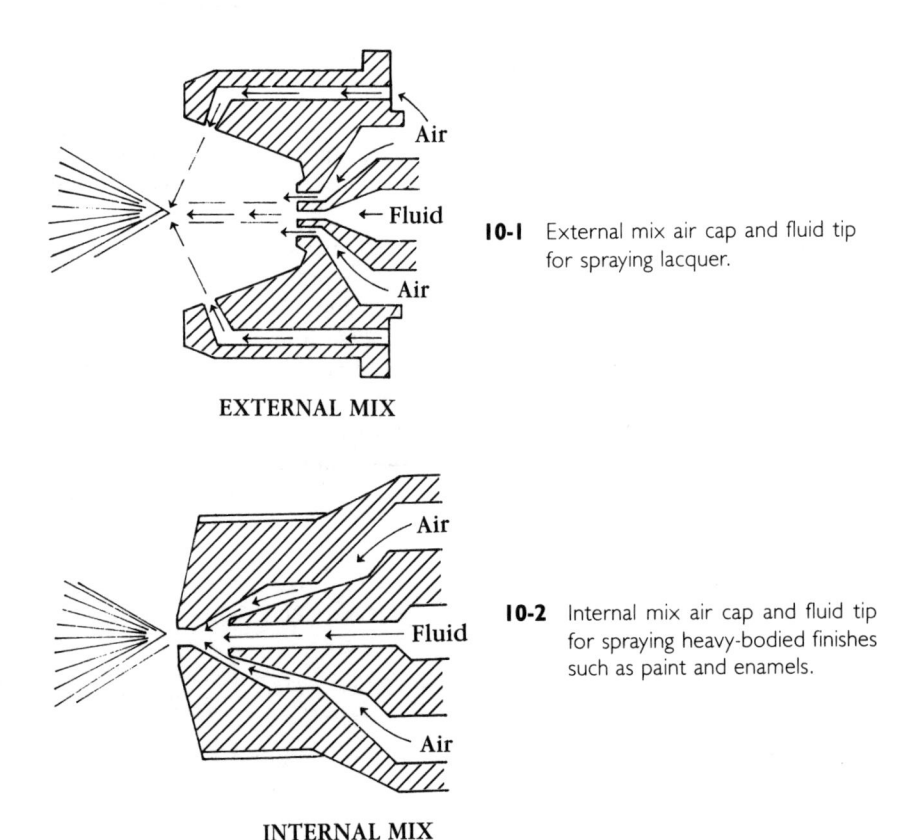

the air when the trigger is released. These guns are used with air compressors that have tanks and pressure-controlling devices. The air compressor shuts off when the tank is full of air.

*Airless spray guns*, or *hydraulic spray systems*, operate by hydraulic pressure. Paint is atomized by forcing paint through a specially shaped nozzle at pressures from 1,000 to 2,500 pounds per square inch. Air is not needed to blow the paint out of the spray gun. Fluid leaving the gun is atomized and floats to the surface it is coating, engulfing it and rarely missing a spot. There is no air to bounce off and distort the spray pattern, and less finish material is wasted. Airless spray guns are used principally by house painters and in factories. Not all airless spray guns work well with lacquer.

## Spray gun selection

Low-quality, inexpensive spray guns do not always properly atomize the finish. They can give small, uneven spray patterns. These guns are suitable to spray houses, fences, and rough surfaces, but not fine lacquer finishes.

- Spray guns to use with *lacquer* and *light-bodied finishes*: vacuum, external-mix, and nonbleeder-type spray guns.

- Spray guns to use with *heavy paint and finishes*: pressure feed and internal-mix spray guns.
- Spray guns to use with *acrylic* and *heavy-bodied paints*: airless spray guns.

### Spray gun adjustment

The *spreader valve* adjusts the size of the spray pattern. Screwing the valve in gives a small ball of finish. Screwing the valve out gives a wide fan of finish. When the fan is adjusted properly, the material will be uniform throughout the fan from top to bottom.

The *air cap* directs the fan of finish that is sprayed out of the gun. Rotating the air cap so its horns are horizontal gives a vertical spray pattern; this is excellent for spraying tabletops. Turning the air cap so the horns are vertical gives a horizontal spray pattern; this is the proper position to spray up and down on cabinets or vertical objects.

The *fluid adjustment screw* controls the amount of finish you spray. Turning the fluid screw in restricts the amount of finish that leaves the spray gun. Turning the screw out provides a full flow of finish out of the gun.

When the spreader valve is set to produce a ball, turn the fluid screw in to decrease the amount of finish being applied. This will prevent runs from excess material. When the spreader is on full fan, turn the fluid screw out for full material flow.

The *material cup* holds finishing material. It is attached to the spray gun and tightened with an attached lever. Keep the small air vent on top of the cup clean and open or little finish will come out of the gun. Do not fill the cup more than 3/4 full; if overfilled, finish might run out the air vent hole on top of the cup and drip onto the project.

Spray gun parts are shown in FIG. 10-3.

### Spray gun handling

To operate the spray gun, hold the gun in your hand. Place two fingers around the trigger; use the index and middle finger. The gun can become heavy during constant operation. Using two fingers on the trigger reduces fatigue on the hand and arm.

When the trigger is pulled, the first stop on the trigger is pure air, no finish. This air can be used to blow dust off the project. As you continue pulling the trigger past the first air stop, finish material is pulled out of the gun and blown onto the project. Always pull the trigger fully on.

### Air hose

To keep the air hose that is attached to the gun from dragging across the wet finish, hold the hose in one hand and the spray gun in the other hand. Hold the hose in front of your body. On large horizontal surfaces where you must lean across the project to reach the opposite side, hold the hose behind your back.

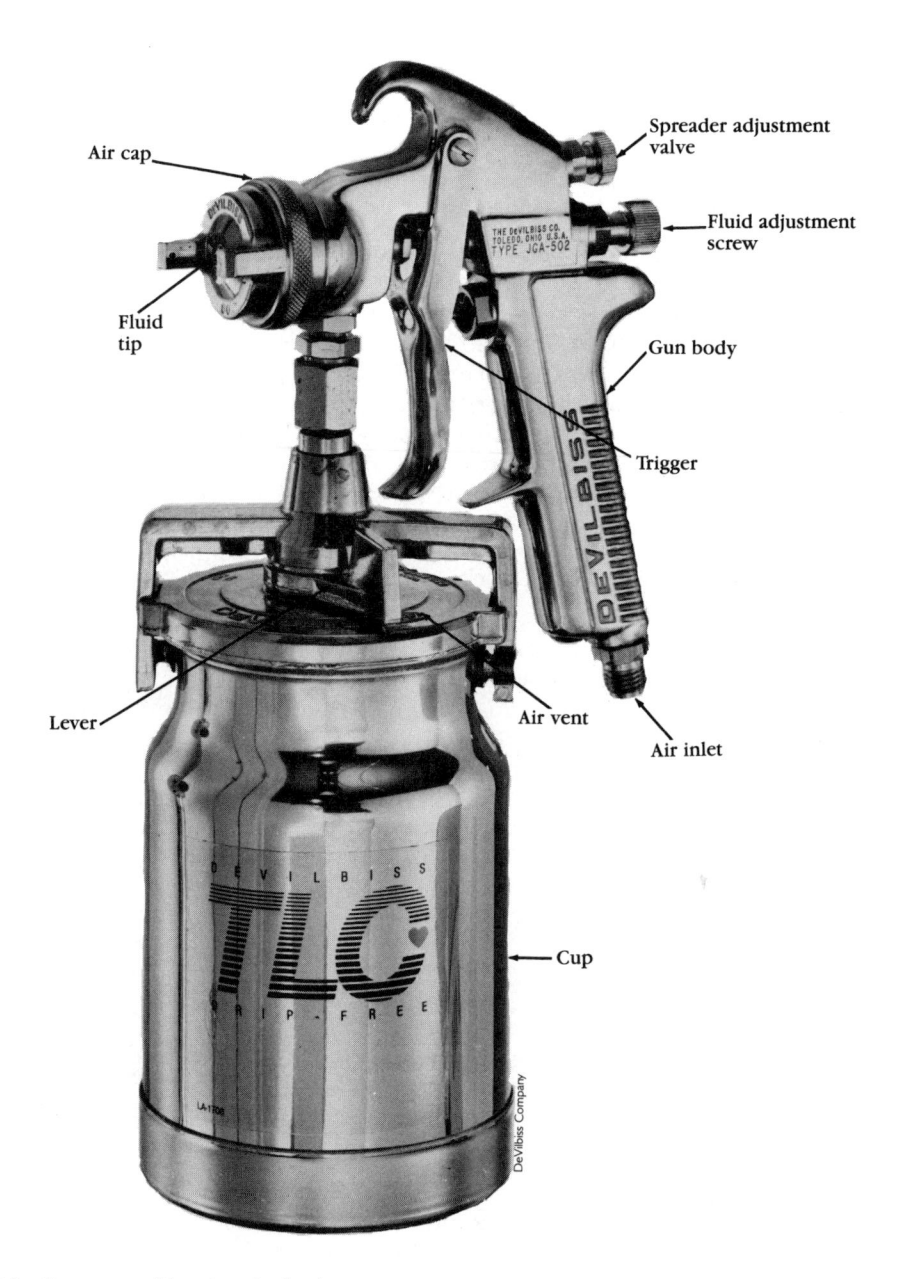

**10-3** Spray gun with external mix air cap.

## Spray gun cleaning

The spray gun must be kept clean. Always clean the gun when you have finished spraying for the day. If the gun is used continuously, stop spraying occasionally and clean the air tip and cup air vent.

To clean the gun, put your finger or a rag over the air cap. At the same time, press a finger over the air vent on the cup cover and pull the trigger. This forces finish out of the gun and back into the cup.

Fill the material cup 1/4 full of lacquer thinner. Attach the cup to the spray gun. Plug the air vent on the cup cover with a finger and shake the gun vigorously, then spray lacquer thinner through the gun.

Soak the air tip in lacquer thinner. Clean the outside of the gun with lacquer thinner. Clean the air vent on cup cover; it is all right to use a nail to unplug the hole.

Do not use metal objects to clean the air cap or fluid tip; use lacquer thinner or a broom straw. Do not soak the entire gun in lacquer thinner because soaking dries out the packing around the trigger needle. Occasionally lubricate the packing around the trigger needle with a drop of oil.

## SPRAYING TECHNIQUES

When spraying vertical surfaces, hold the gun perpendicular to the surface, about 6 to 10 inches away. When spraying downward on horizontal surfaces, hold the gun at a 60-degree angle. This position prevents finish from running out of the air vent on the cup cover and dripping onto the project.

Hold the gun outside the object being coated. As the gun moves toward the project, just before reaching the surface, pull the trigger all the way. Move the gun at a constant speed and distance across and off the surface, then release the trigger and stop spraying. Start the second stroke by fully pulling the trigger just before reaching the surface, overlapping the first coat by 50 percent. Continue on across the project, releasing the trigger as you pass off the surface. Spray back and forth until the surface is evenly coated.

It is important that the gun be moved at a constant speed and held at a constant distance (6 to 10 inches away). Never start or stop spraying while the gun is over the surface, or you will have heavy blobs of finish and bare spots. Do not arc the gun from side to side, or the finish will be thick in the center and thin on the edges.

Try to spray even, wet coats following the grain of the wood. If the gun is too far away or moved too fast, the coat will be thin and might look uneven and sandy. If the gun is held too close or moved too slowly, you will have a thick coat, and the finish might run or sag. Lap each spraying stroke halfway over the preceding stroke to ensure an even finish.

Spray hard-to-reach inside surfaces first and inside of legs and cabinets; then spray the lower vertical surfaces. Spray horizontal surfaces last. When spraying level surfaces, tabletops, chair seats, or other flat surfaces, spray around the outer edges first. Then, with the gun at a 60-degree angle following the grain of the wood, spray from the near to the far side of the top. The exhaust fan will pull overspray away from the wet surface, decreasing the collection of spray dust on the freshly sprayed surface. Refer to FIG. 10-4 for proper spraying procedures.

You must stop often and clean the air vent on the spray gun cup

**100** Lacquer finishing

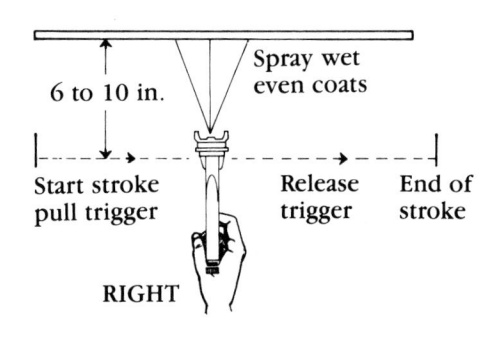

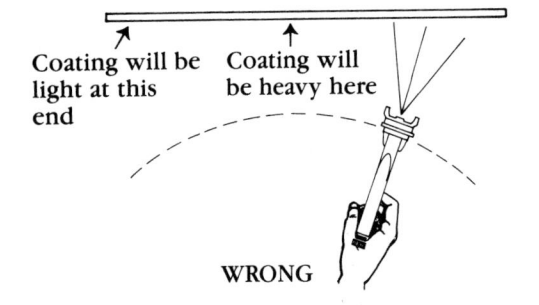

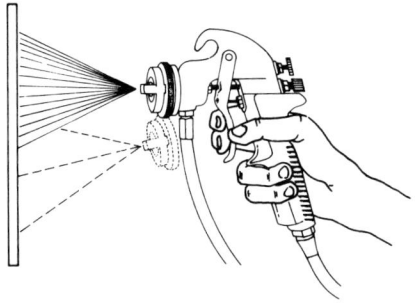

6 to 10 in.
Spray wet even coats
Start stroke pull trigger
Release trigger
End of stroke
**RIGHT**

Coating will be light at this end
Coating will be heavy here
**WRONG**

Hold the gun perpendicular to the surface. Tilting (dotted lines) will result in an uneven pattern

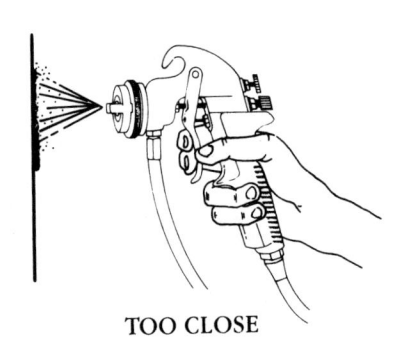

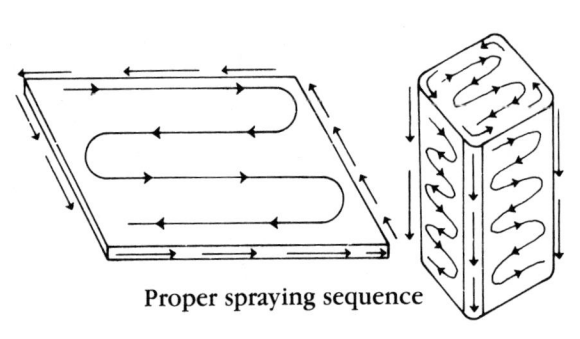

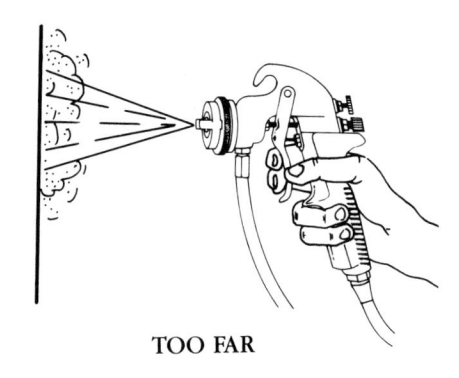

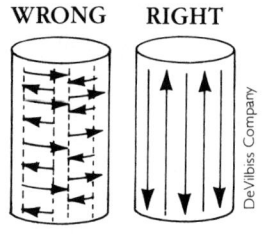

**TOO CLOSE**

**TOO FAR**

Proper spraying sequence

**WRONG** **RIGHT**

Small round objects need at least three strokes to cover

DeVilbiss Company

**10-4** Spray finishing techniques.

*Spraying techniques* **101**

**10-4** Continued.

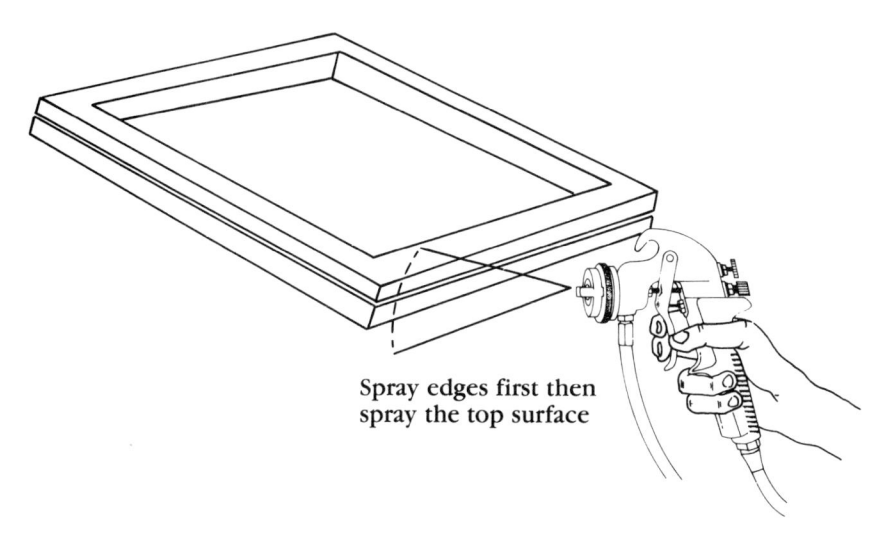

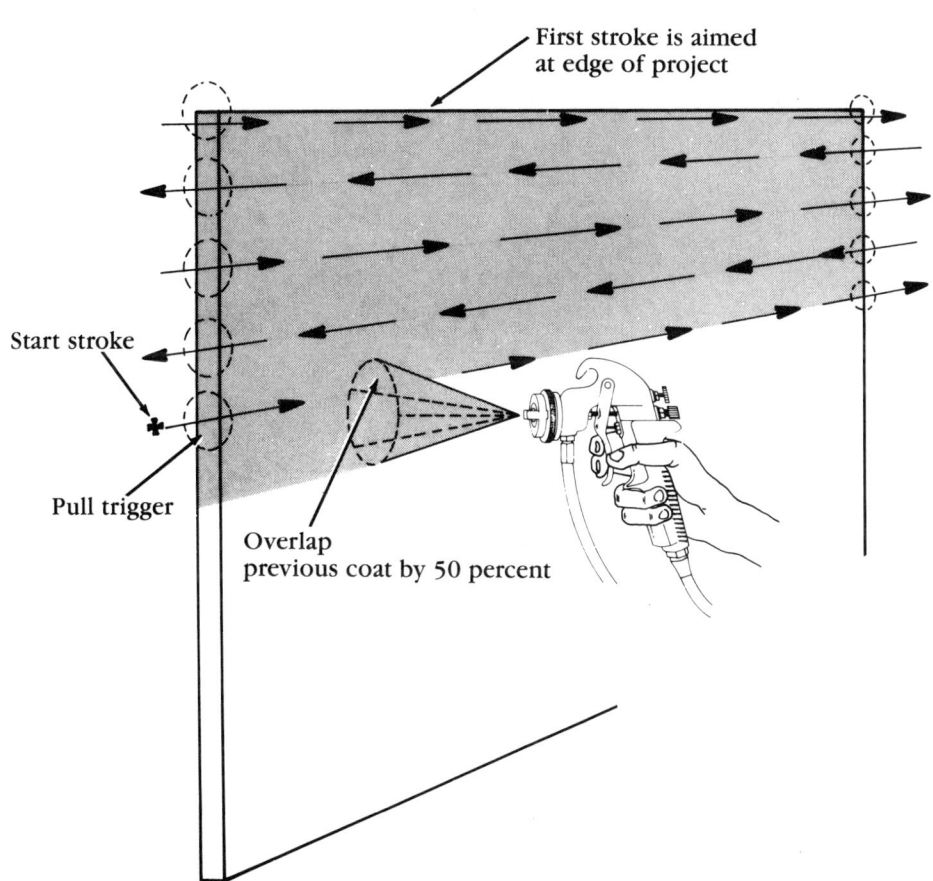

Spray edges first then spray the top surface

First stroke is aimed at edge of project

Start stroke

Pull trigger

Overlap previous coat by 50 percent

102   Lacquer finishing

## FAULTY PATTERNS and how to correct them

| PATTERN | CAUSE | CORRECTION |
|---------|-------|------------|
|  | Dried material in side-port "A" restricts passage of air. Greater flow of air from cleaner side-port "B" forces fan pattern in direction of clogged side. | Dissolve material in side-ports with thinner, then blow gun clean. Do not poke into openings with metal instruments. |
|  | Dried material around the outside of the fluid nozzle tip at position "C" restricts the passage of atomizing air at one point through the center opening of air nozzle and results in pattern shown. This pattern can also be caused by loose air nozzle. | Remove air nozzle and wipe off fluid tip, using rag wet with thinner. Tighten air nozzle. |

# Spraying techniques

| Pattern | Cause | Correction |
|---|---|---|
| (split spray shape) | A split spray or one that is heavy on each end of a fan pattern and weak in the middle is usually caused by (1) too high an atomization air pressure, or (2) by attempting to get too wide a spray with thin material. | Reducing air pressure will correct cause (1). To correct cause (2), open material control to full position by turning to left. At the same time, turn spray width adjustment to right. This will reduce width of spray but will correct split spray pattern. |
| SPITTING (spitting pattern shape) | (1) Dried out packing around material needle valve permits air to get into fluid passageway. This results in spitting. (2) Dirt between fluid nozzle seat and body or loosely installed fluid nozzle will make gun spit. (3) A loose or defective swivel nut on siphon cup or material hose can cause spitting. | To correct cause (1) back up knurled nut (E), place two drops of machine oil on packing, replace nut and tighten with fingers only. In aggravated cases, replace packing.<br><br>To correct cause (2), remove fluid nozzle (F), clean back of nozzle and nozzle seat in gun body using rag wet with thinner, replace nozzle and draw up tightly against body.<br><br>To correct cause (3), tighten or replace swivel nut. |

**10-5** Correcting problem spray patterns.

BINKS Manufacturing Company

cover. If it becomes plugged, no material will come out of the gun. Also clean the air cap and fluid tip on the spray gun often. If they become plugged with finish, the spray fan will be distorted and the flow of finish restricted. Use lacquer thinner to clean the gun. Common spray problems are shown in FIG. 10-5.

## SAFETY

- Avoid breathing spray dust or fumes from overspray.
- Do not spray near fire, sparks, cigarettes, or gas water heaters.
- If finishing material splashes in your eyes, immediately flush your eyes with water.
- Wash hands before eating or touching your mouth. If your hands or skin has lacquer on them, clean it off with lacquer thinner, then dry and wash them with soap and water.
- Place the project being sprayed between you and the exhaust fan. This arrangement allows overspray to be pulled away from your face.
- Fumes and overspray dust is not healthy to breathe. Wear a dust mask. A dust mask will filter out finish particles suspended in the air and keep them out of your lungs.
- *A note of caution*: dust masks will not filter out fumes from spraying. When spraying finishing materials in a confined area without cross-ventilation, you must wear a respirator with charcoal filters to remove the fumes. Paint stores sell respirators with charcoal filters.

## LACQUER FINISH

To obtain a smooth, level finish on wood, three or more coats of lacquer sanding sealer must be sprayed on the surface prior to applying the satin or gloss top finish coats.

Lacquer sanding sealer is a high solid sealer that builds up fast, filling pores and small dents. Lacquer dries fast and is easy to sand.

Sanding sealer is good to fill pores and seal the wood, but it is not a durable finish and does not wear well. A more durable finish is sprayed over the sealer—gloss lacquer for a high-gloss shiny finish, satin lacquer for a semigloss finish, or flat lacquer for a dull finish.

Top coats of lacquer, gloss, or satin should be applied over lacquer sanding sealer. Lacquer top coats are hard to sand. They sink into the woods pores rather than filling them. Several coats must be applied to build up a thick lacquer film. Top coats can be used as first coats, but they are not good sealers. Lacquer sanding sealer should be used first to fill pores and provide a smooth level surface for top coats to lie on.

## LACQUER FINISH APPLICATIONS

Lacquer finish coats dry quickly. This rapid drying time enables the finisher to use several finishing steps in a relatively short time—glazing, shading, distressing, plus sealer and top coat applications. These finishing methods can be accomplished with the piece dry and ready to rub in two warm days, 70 degrees or more, or in one day with forced drying, using drying rooms or heat lamps.

### Simple lacquer finish

*Materials*

Lacquer sanding sealer

Lacquer top coats (flat, satin, or gloss)

Lacquer thinner

Paint strainer or nylon stocking

400-grit wet or dry sandpaper

Tack rag

Air compressor and spray gun

Spray dust mask

*Application*

1. Sand the wood smooth and stain it (optional).
2. Spray one coat of lacquer sanding sealer. Thin with 50 percent lacquer thinner. Dry about 30 minutes at 70 degrees.
3. Spray one double coat of lacquer sanding sealer. Thin with 30 percent lacquer thinner. Spray one wet coat and immediately follow with a second wet coat. Dries in 1 hour at 70 degrees.
4. Sand with 400-grit sandpaper. Clean the sanded surface with a tack rag.
5. Spray one coat of gloss, satin, or flat lacquer. Strain through a paint strainer or nylon. Thin with 30 percent lacquer thinner. Dries in 1 hour at 70 degrees.
6. Sand off dust spots with 400-grit sandpaper. Use water or paint thinner as a lubricant. Clean the sanded surface with a tack rag.
7. Spray a final coat of strained gloss, satin, or flat lacquer. Thin with 30 percent lacquer thinner.
8. Dry for 48 hours.
9. Rub as needed.

### Complex lacquer finish

*Materials*

Lacquer sanding sealer

Lacquer top coats (flat, satin, or gloss)

Lacquer thinner

Strainer or nylon stocking

400-grit wet or dry sandpaper

Sandpaper block

280-grit sandpaper

Oil color

Paint thinner

Soft cotton cloth (to glaze extra color on finish)

Stiff-bristle brush or toothbrush (to make antique marks)

Shading lacquer

Air compressor and spray gun

Spray dust respirator

Tack rag

*Application*

1. Sand the wood smooth and stain it. Apply pore filler (optional step).
2. Spray one coat of lacquer sanding sealer. Thin with 50 percent lacquer thinner.
3. Spray one double coat of lacquer sanding sealer. Thin with 30 percent lacquer thinner.
4. Sand with 400-grit sandpaper.
5. Glaze with color (optional step).
6. If glaze was applied, spray one coat of lacquer sanding sealer. Thin with 30 percent lacquer thinner.
7. Lightly sand with 400-grit sandpaper.
8. Apply distress marks (optional step).
9. If distress marks are applied, spray one coat of lacquer sanding sealer. Thin with 30 percent lacquer thinner.
10. Lightly sand with 400-grit sandpaper
11. Apply shading lacquer (optional step).
12. Spray one coat of lacquer sanding sealer. Thin with 30 percent lacquer thinner.
13. Lightly sand with 400-grit sandpaper.
14. Spray one coat of strained gloss, satin, or flat lacquer. Thin with 30 percent lacquer thinner.
15. Sand lightly with 400-grit sandpaper. Use water or paint thinner as a lubricant.
16. Spray the last coat of strained lacquer, gloss, satin, or flat. Thin with 30 percent lacquer thinner.
17. Dry 48 hours, then rub the finish (optional step).

*Detailed application*

1. First, sand the wood smooth and stain it. Oil color stains can be used. If liquid pore filler is used (optional step, see Chapter 8), spray one coat lacquer sanding sealer thinned with 50 percent lacquer thinner. When dry, apply filler.
2. Spray the stained, or stained and filled, surface with lacquer sanding sealer thinned with 50 percent lacquer thinner. This first thin sealer coat will seal the stain and filler, if any is used, and allow air in the pores to escape without leaving air bubbles in the finish. This thin coat should dry in 30 minutes at 70 degrees.
3. Apply one double coat of sanding sealer thinned with 30 percent lacquer thinner. Spray one wet coat of sealer and, immediately before the first coat dries, follow with a second wet coat of sealer. Watch for and wipe off runs on vertical surfaces. This double coat should dry in one hour at 70 degrees.
4. Sand off dust spots with 400-grit sandpaper. Be careful not to sand through into the stain.
5. Glaze color over the finish to give depth, extra color, or a grain pattern. Use color in oil mixed in paint thinner (see *Glazing* in Chapter 7). The glaze color is dry and ready to be sprayed over when it turns dull.
6. Spray one coat of sealer over the glaze color. Thin with 30 percent lacquer thinner.
7. Lightly sand with 400-grit sandpaper.
8. If distressing is desired, flick small specks of dark color onto the finish (see antique marks in this chapter). These dark spots simulate worm holes and dirt spots, and give an appearance of age. Use black or a dark color in oil mixed with paint thinner. Dip a stiff bristle brush or toothbrush into the color; tap it against a hard surface over the finish or flick the brush with a finger. Small droplets of color will fly off the brush onto the finish.
9. Spray one coat of sealer over the antique spots. Thin with 30 percent lacquer thinner. Dry for one hour at 70 degrees.
10. Lightly sand with 400-grit sandpaper.
11. Lightly spray colored lacquer (shading lacquer) around the edges of flat surfaces and the bulbous parts of turnings. This extra color gives a picture frame effect. It can uniform the color or give dark accents on turnings. Shading color is made by mixing stain color or color in oil with lacquer (see shading in this chapter).
12. Spray one coat of sealer over the shading lacquer. Thin with 30 percent lacquer thinner. Dry for 1 hour at 70 degrees.
13. Sand smooth with 400-grit sandpaper.

14. If gloss lacquer is to be used as top coats, clean the sanded surface with a tack rag. Whisk it across the surface lightly. Do not scrub.
15. Spray one coat of strained gloss satin or flat lacquer thinned with 30 percent lacquer thinner. Dry for one hour at 70 degrees.
16. Lightly sand off dust spots with 400-grit sandpaper. Use water or paint thinner as a lubricant.
17. Clean the surface with a tack rag. Spray the last coat of lacquer thinned with 30 percent lacquer thinner. Strain lacquer through a paint strainer or nylon.
18. If satin or flat lacquer was used as a final coat, it is not necessary to rub the finish. If gloss lacquer was used or if you wish to change the finish's sheen, rub the surface. Allow to dry for 48 hours before rubbing (see *Hand-Rubbed Finishes*, Chapter 13).

Because there are variations in viscosity between different brands of lacquer, you might have to increase or decrease the amount of lacquer thinner that is suggested.

To obtain a smooth glass-like surface on wood that has deep pores, use liquid pore filler or lacquer sanding sealer to fill the cell cavities. If you use a lacquer sanding sealer as a filler, apply several coats of sealer and sand smooth. Repeat steps three and four in the complex lacquer finish application. Experienced finishers use 280-grit sandpaper with a sandpaper block to speed this sanding. Because 280-grit paper cuts fast, care must be taken to avoid sanding through the sealer.

## TYPES OF LACQUERS

*Clear gloss lacquer* is a clear glossy finish, thinned with lacquer thinner. It is applied by spraying and is used as a final top coat. Apply it over lacquer sanding sealer.

*Clear flat* or *satin lacquer* is the same as clear gloss lacquer, except it dries with a dull sheen.

*Lacquer enamel* is lacquer with color added. Use it as a top coat.

*Lacquer sanding sealer* is a heavy-bodied sealer that is used for first coats. It fills pores, seals stain and filler, and is easy to sand. Clear lacquer top coats must be sprayed over sanding sealer.

*Brushing lacquer* is a slow-drying lacquer that is formulated to be brushed.

*Alcohol-resistant lacquer* is a tough, durable lacquer that is resistant to alcohol.

*Water white lacquer* is a highly transparent lacquer that will not yellow or darken when used over blond or light-colored finishes.

*Shading lacquer* is a lacquer with color added. It is sprayed over finishes to darken, color, or add highlights.

*Acrylic lacquer* is a tough, water-resistant lacquer used to coat metal patio furniture or automobiles.

*Leather lacquer* is a flexible lacquer used to spray over leather.

*Novelty lacquers* are Wrinkle Lacquers (small wrinkles cover the surface of this lacquer) and Frost Lacquers (looks like frost on a window).

*Lacquer thinner* is a volatile solvent used to thin lacquer. It also is a mild remover used to clean brushes or wood after using paint remover. Lacquer thinner spilled on a finish will ruin it.

## DISTRESSING

Some factory-finished pieces are covered with distress marks, simulated worm holes, dents, dark spots, scratches, and blemishes. These marks are applied with drills, denting tools, rasps, and spray guns that spit out small dark spots of color. The purpose is to make a piece of furniture look old and resemble a worn antique.

You can make your own antique marks with some simple tools. Prior to finishing, drill small holes in the wood. Concentrate on one area because worms tend to feed on one spot, not the entire piece. Antiques have rounded edges from long use. Sandpaper or rasp high wear areas, edges, corners, and chair rungs. Make dents and gouges by striking bare wood with a hammer, chains, ice pick, or any sharp object. Lightly sand over these distressed areas before finishing, but do not remove them.

### Antique marks

Antique marks are applied to partially finished pieces prior to applying the final finish coats. Dark color is flicked or spattered on the finish to simulate worm holes, dirt spots, and blemishes, and to give the appearance of age. Black, Vandyke brown, burnt umber, and raw umber are colors that are often used.

Dip a stiff bristle brush or toothbrush into the thinned color and tap the brush against a hard surface over the finish (FIG. 10-6) or flick the brush. To flick, bend the bristles back with your thumb and release. The bristles will spring back, throwing color specks onto the surface. Spray cans that spray antique spots are available from finish supply dealers.

**10-6** Antique marks.

Once antique marks are applied, continue with the finishing process (see complex finish application in this chapter).

## Marking

Usually in conjunction with applying antique spots, small curved lines 1/8 to 1/2 inch long are also applied. The marks are random in pattern, shape, and length. The purpose is to simulate old scratches that have darkened with age. Special graining pencils are made to apply the marks, but a fine brush or sharp-pointed stick dipped in color works as well, as shown in FIG. 10-7.

10-7 Marking—simulating old scratches.

## Shading with lacquer

Shading is accomplished by lightly spraying colored lacquer (shading lacquer) around the edges of flat surfaces, usually tabletops. It is also used to uniform the color of a piece when the parts are not the same color. The valleys of bulbous parts of turnings on the tables and chairs are slightly dark-ended to give contrast. Shading can make a dull, uninteresting piece look richer and like it had been professionally finished. An aerosol is used to shade the edges of a table top in FIG. 10-8.

Most finish suppliers sell shading lacquer, which is lacquer with color added. Make your own shading lacquer by adding oil color to lacquer. Color the lacquer slightly darker than the stain that was used on the piece. Add lacquer thinner to make the mixture spray freely.

A small shading gun is excellent to spray shading lacquer. You can control the shading gun by triggering (lightly pressing the trigger) to give a fine mist or a wet coat. The spray pattern can be adjusted to a fine point

**10-8** Shading—adding color around the edges of tops.

or a fan. It makes the application of color precise because color goes where you want it. Shading guns are excellent, but any lacquer spray gun will work. When you use full-size spray guns, you lose some control of finish application. Aerosol spray cans can also be used. Lightly dust shading lacquer around edges, graduating the overspray in toward the center of the top. A small amount of color is fogged toward the center. Avoid dark lines or rings of color.

Lightly shade around the edges of flat surfaces, tabletops, and chair seats. Also shade chair backs, aprons, and the valleys of bulbous turnings on chair and table legs.

Go easy. Dust the color; avoid dark blobs or streaks. The color should look natural and part of the finish (see complex lacquer finish in this chapter).

## FINISH PROBLEMS

### Cracking crazing

**Cause** (1) The finish has dried out. (2) Hard, inelastic finish applied over softer finish.

**Cure** *Lacquer finish*—remelt finish with lacquer thinner; spray or brush on. Soak cracked finish with lacquer thinner until the old finish flows out and the cracks disappear. When the finish flows out (reamalgamates), apply two or more coats of lacquer sanding sealer; sand between coats. When smooth, apply top coats of satin or gloss lacquer.

*Varnish finish*—Remelt finish with a varnish amalgamator. When dry, sand and revarnish. Varnish amalgamator softens varnish, allowing it to flow out and fill in the cracks.

## Fish eyes and holes

Small round holes that appear in the finish when spraying are called fish eyes and holes.

**Cause** Silicone in furniture polish is on or has penetrated through the finish and soaked into the wood. Small holes appear when finish is applied over the silicone (FIG. 10-9). Washing or stripping the finish off the wood does not remove silicone. It is difficult to remove.

**10-9** Fish eyes—the finish pulls away from silicone that is in the wood and forms small holes.

**Cure** Add several drops of liquid silicone (smoothie), a fish eye retarder, and extra thinner to the finish. Immediately, before the first coat with fish eyes dries, respray the wet surface with a heavy, wet coat of finish and smoothie. The fish eyes should flow out and disappear. If the finish dries before you are able to recoat, sand the finish and fish eyes smooth, or wash off the finish and recoat using silicone in the new finish.

Too much silicone added to a finish can cause it to turn milky or hazy, and the surface will have a slick, oily film. Spraying several coats of finish with silicone added can also cause this problem. Add the silicone to your finish sparingly, just enough to make the fish eyes flow out and disappear. Some finishers add silicone to their finishes each time they refinish a piece. This is not a good practice. Silicone should only be added when it is known there is silicone on the piece or when fish eyes appear. Often one coat of finish with silicone added is enough to seal the fish eyes; subsequent coats might not need silicone added to them.

**Cause** Wax, oil, or grease is on the finish or wood.
**Cure** Clean finishes prior to finishing with paint thinner. Clean wood with lacquer thinner.

### Finish peeling

**Cause** (1) Finish not compatible with undercoats. (2) Silicones from polishes loosening finish from wood. (3) Water damage. (4) Parquet surfaces. Finish tends to pull away from joints where parquet meet when wet with water or impregnated with silicone.

**Cure** *Lacquer finish*—remelt the finish with lacquer thinner; soak the finish with lacquer thinner until finish melts back onto the wood. Touch up light spots; puddle low spots with lacquer sanding sealer where finish is missing. When the sealer dries, sand the hardened puddled spots. Coat with lacquer sanding sealer. Sand between coats and apply gloss or flat lacquer.

*Varnish* or *urethane finish*—remove the old finish with paint remover and refinish.

### Pinholes

Small pin-size holes appear in the finish.

**Cause** The finish begins to harden before the thinners evaporate. Solvent gases escape as small bubbles leaving *pinholes*.

**Cure** When the finish dries, sand and recoat with finish. Reduce air pressure and add the correct ratio of thinner.

### Finish rough, sandy, or pebbly

**Cause** (1) Finish too thick; (2) spray gun held too far from work; (3) air pressure too high. (4) Refer to FIG. 10-5.

**Cure** Sand finish smooth and recoat with a wet finish coat.

### Runs

**Cause** (1) Spraying too close; (2) moving the gun too slow; (3) material too thin.

**Cure** Refer to FIG. 10-4.

### Spray gun clogged

Spray material will not come out of gun (this is a common spray problem).

**Cause** (1) Air vent on the cup cover is clogged or air cap or fluid tip is dirty; (2) spray material too thick; (3) air pressure too low.

**Cure** Refer to FIG. 10-5.

### Streaks

**Cause** (1) Finish not being applied evenly; (2) gun held too far from work; (3) gun moved too fast; (4) finish material too thick; (5) air pressure too high; (6) not overlapping spray strokes 50 percent; or (7) fluid tip, air cap, or air vent on cup is dirty.

**Cure** Refer to FIGS. 10-4 and 10-5.

## Wet finish

Finish does not dry, or there are shiny, sticky spots.

**Cause** (1) Wax from paint remover was not properly cleaned off the wood when the finish was removed; or (2) there is grease or oil on the wood.

**Cure** Gently rub wet spots on the finish with a rag dampened with paint thinner or water. When wet spots dry or turn white, recoat with finish. This might need to be done several times.

## Finish turns white

**Cause** (1) Stain in the wood was not dry when finish was applied; (2) finish applied over wet paint thinner or solvent; (3) high humidity (avoid spraying when it is raining or the humidity is high); or (4) fast-drying, inexpensive lacquer thinner will cause lacquer to turn white when spraying in cold, damp weather. Add blush retarder or use slow-drying, quality lacquer thinner.

**Cure** When the finish dries, recoat with finish. When finishing in high humidity, add a blush retarder to the finish.

# Chapter 11
# Finishing unfinished furniture

When searching for furniture to finish, don't overlook new unfinished furniture. These unfinished or "nude" pieces can be finished to look as good as factory-finished furniture, and they are usually reasonably priced. Because there are no finishing costs added to the piece, the price to you is reduced, making it more affordable. Nude furniture is sold by specialty furniture stores and through department store catalogues. These stores often sell finishing materials and can give you advice on how to use them.

Furniture made in home workshops or pieces made to your specifications by a professional cabinetmaker also need finishing. Not all cabinetmakers are good at applying finishes. You can probably put on a better finish than the cabinetmaker, plus save on the finishing costs.

Several grades of nude furniture can be purchased, from quality cherry, oak, and birch hardwood pieces to inexpensive pine and fir items. Nude furniture is assembled and sanded. Unlike working on a piece with an existing finish, nude furniture does not have an old finish to remove. On quality nude pieces, cabinet repairs should not be necessary, and only minor sanding is required.

Inexpensive nude pine and fir will probably require some cabinet repairs. Joints are not always tight, and there might be gaps in them. Figures 11-1 and 11-2 show a loose door frame and a split side that will need gluing. Drawer faces might be loose from their sides. Brad and nail holes often need to be filled with putty. There will probably be small dents that should be sanded out. Knots in nude pine furniture might be loose or oozing sap. The sap must be cleaned off and the knot sealed. Loose knots must be glued and filled (FIGS. 11-3, 11-4, and 11-5). Bargain pieces might not be bargains if too much work is required to make them presentable. It is better to pay a little more and buy a quality hardwood item.

116   *Finishing unfinished furniture*

**11-1**  Loose door frame.

**11-2**  Split side post.

**11-3**  Loose knot hole.

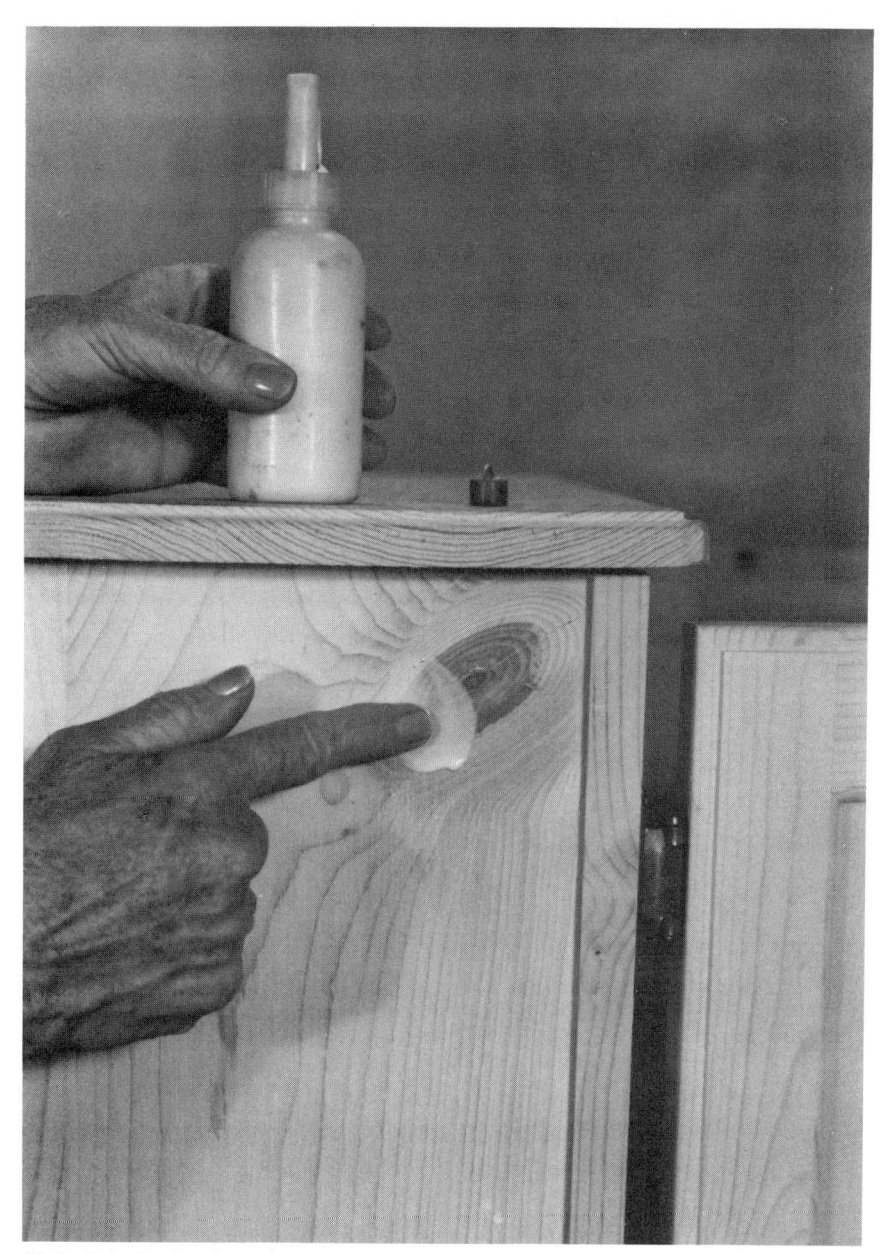

**11-4** Rub glue into loose knots.

If your plan is to paint or antique your piece with a solid color, use an inexpensive pine or fir cabinet. The opaque color will hide the wood and its imperfections. If the piece you are finishing is constructed with a hardwood like oak, cherry, or birch, use a clear finish that will show off the fine wood grain. Finishes that can be used are varnish, urethane, lacquer, and penetrating sealer finishes.

**11-5** Push putty into the loose split.

## CHOOSING THE FINISH

Before selecting the finish for your project, ask yourself how the piece will be used, then choose the finish accordingly. If the item is to be used in the family room, kitchen, or by children, select a tough durable urethane that can be brushed or sprayed. For a fine finish on living room or bedroom furniture, consider brushing varnish on the piece or spraying it with lacquer.

If you want a contemporary Danish-type finish, use a penetrating resin sealer finish. Penetrating sealer finishes can be purchased clear or with stain colors added.

Refer to Chapter 1 for a detailed description of finishes.

## CABINET PREPARATION

Before applying the finish, check the cabinet for construction defects. Glue all loose joints (FIGS. 11-6 and 11-7). Fill nail holes, gaps in joints, and dings with wood putty (FIG. 11-8). Glue and nail loose joints on drawers. Wax the drawer guides and runners; they must be firmly attached and the drawers must work smoothly in and out of the case (FIG. 11-9). Nail furniture glides to the bottom of the cabinet (FIG. 11-10).

11-6 Glue and clamp a split on the side.

### Sealing sap

If sap is oozing out of knots or pores on pine furniture, it must be removed. Scrape it off with a razor blade, then wash the piece clean with paint thinner. Seal the cleaned sap areas with shellac to stop the sap from reappearing.

When shellac is used as a sealer, the piece might need to be antiqued or finished over with an opaque color. Once shellac is applied, the wood usually cannot be stained.

**120** *Finishing unfinished furniture*

**11-7** Reglue the loose frame.

**11-8** Fill nail and brad holes with putty.

**11-9** For smooth operation, rub wax on the bottom edges and center guides of drawers.

**11-10** Furniture glides protect the base from splitting when moving the cabinet across the floor.

## Sanding

Use sandpaper and a sandpaper block to sand out dents and scratches that are on the wood. Sand off dried putty that you applied or any glue that might be on the wood (FIG. 11-11).

**11-11** An electric hand sander speeds sanding.

Lightly smooth and round the sharp edges and corners on tops of cabinets and tables with sandpaper and a sandpaper block (FIG. 11-12). If the furniture is to be used by children, increase the rounding. A sharp edge or corner can injure children if they fall against it.

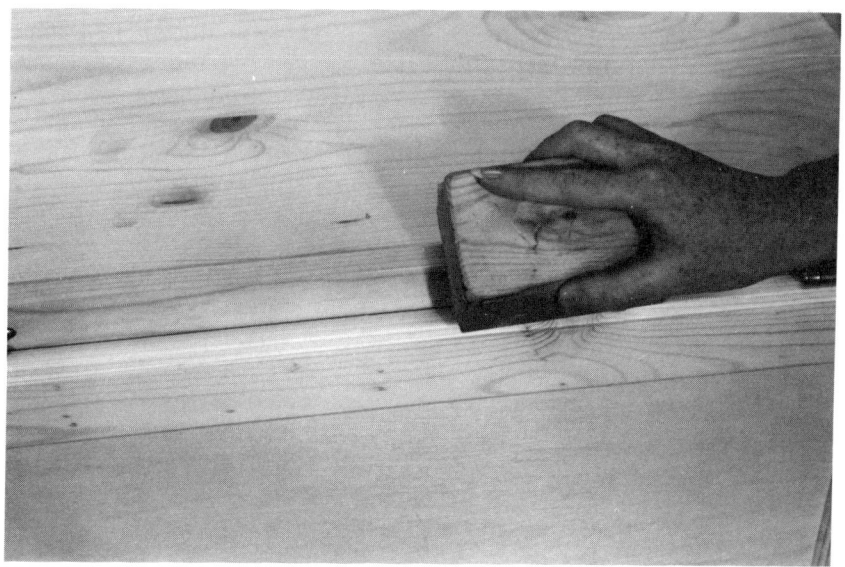

**11-12** Round off all sharp edges. Use a sandpaper block and sandpaper.

Glue down slivers or cut off and sand them smooth (FIG. 11-13). If the void left by a removed sliver is too large to sand out, fill the void with putty; when the putty dries, sand it smooth. Sand with the grain of the wood. Cross-grain scratches from sandpaper are difficult to sand off and will stand out when the wood is stained. See Chapter 5 for sanding instructions.

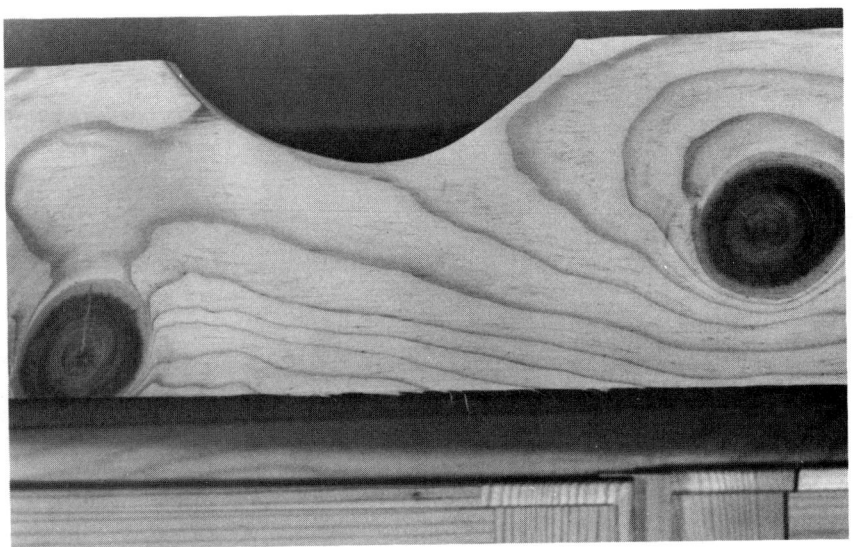

**11-13** Sand rough edges on the bottom of drawers smooth.

## Staining

The next step after sanding is to apply a stain. Most woods have little color and need a stain to color the wood and bring out the grain pattern. Stains that are easy to use and easy to find are premixed oil colors, artist's oil colors in tubes, and sealing stains that seal the wood and stain at the same time.

Test the stain you select on an obscure part of the project or on a scrap of wood. If the color is right, continue staining. If the color is not what you want, try another color until you find the proper color.

I prefer to use artist's oil colors. When mixed with paint thinner, they can be blended to match most furniture colors. For large projects, I prefer quart cans of oil colors.

Apply the stain with a soft cotton cloth. Completely cover one surface at a time—side, front, or top (FIG. 11-14). Force stain into the grooves with the stain rag or a soft brush that is wet with color (FIG. 11-15). Wipe off excess stain with a cotton cloth, following the grain of the wood. Cotton diapers make good staining and cleaning rags.

When the stain dries on the wood it turns dull and looks dead, so you might be tempted to restain the piece. Don't! When the finish is applied, the color will come back to life and look beautiful. See Chapter 7, *Staining instructions*.

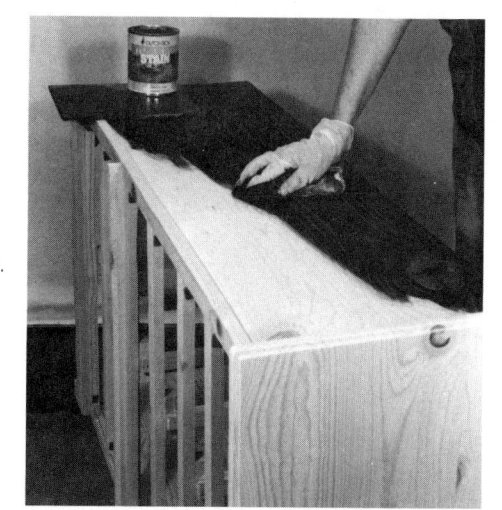

**11-14** Apply an even coat of oil stain.

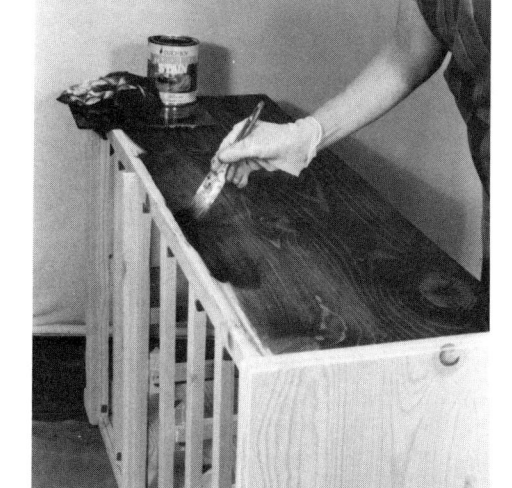

**11-15** Push stain into corners with a brush.

## APPLYING THE FINISH

The project is now ready to be coated with a clear finish. Use sealer on new wood to fill pores and seal the wood. The sealer provides a smooth, level surface for top coats to lie on. Apply one coat of sealer to all surfaces on drawers, inside, bottom, and sides. Also apply one coat of sealer to the inside of cabinets. Sometimes the insides of cabinets are hard to reach but are worth the effort. Unfinished surfaces can absorb moisture, causing the wood to swell and eventually to warp and crack. This coat of sealer will reduce warping and splitting.

If you chose varnish as the finish, brush on two coats of varnish sanding sealer. Sand between coats, using 400-grit wet or dry sandpaper with water; then brush on two coats of satin or gloss varnish. If you do not use sanding sealer, apply two to three coats of varnish (FIG. 11-16).

11-16 Brush two to three coats of finish over the dried stain.

When spray equipment is available, you can use a lacquer finish. Spray three coats of lacquer sanding sealer over the stained wood. Gently sand the sealer with 400-grit wet or dry sandpaper and water; then spray two coats of satin or gloss lacquer over the sealer.

For a durable urethane finish, brush or spray two to three coats of satin or gloss urethane over the wood.

Earlier in this chapter I said that penetrating sealers are the easiest finishes to use. You wipe them on, then wipe them off. Penetrating finishes that can be used are commercially prepared penetrating sealers with or without stain colors, tung oil, and linseed oil. I prefer the commercially prepared penetrating sealer, with tung oil as a second choice.

Stain the wood or use a penetrating sealer that has color added. Apply three coats, flooding the wood with oil. When the wood stops absorbing the finish, wipe it dry. Three coats will give you a flat Danish-type in-the-wood finish.

## Enameling

Pieces that are to be painted with a solid color or antiqued should first be coated with a clear sealer. Sealers seal the wood, fill pores, and give a smooth surface for top coats to lie on. A clear sealer under a painted finish will keep paint out of pores. This is important because if you decide to remove the paint later and refinish the piece to a natural wood finish, the pores will be free of colored paint. It is very difficult to remove paint from pores.

Use varnish sanding sealer under a colored varnish-type enamel. Use lacquer sanding sealer when a colored lacquer enamel is sprayed. Urethane enamels require sealers specified by the manufacturer. Follow the instructions on the container.

To apply the enamel finish, brush or spray on two coats of sealer, sanding between coats. Follow with two coats of colored enamel. Refer to Chapter 9, *Applying finishes*, for finish application instructions.

### Antiquing

To obtain an antiqued finish, lightly glaze oil color over the final coat of the enamel with a rag wet with oil color. Following the grain of the wood, leave uniform lines of color on top of the enamel. Later, when the glaze color dries, coat the piece with a clear finish to protect the glaze. Use clear satin or gloss varnish for varnish-type enamels, clear lacquer for lacquer enamels, and clear urethane for urethane enamels. See ''Glazing'' and ''Antiquing'' in Chapter 7.

After the final coat of finish has been applied and dried, stand back and take a close look at your project. If the finish is smooth and looks good to you, the piece is finished and ready for you to attach the handles (FIG. 11-17).

**11-17** Attach handles after the finish has been applied and rubbed.

If the surface is rough with runs and objectionable brush lines, sand the finish smooth and recoat with finish. Another option is to sand the rough surface smooth and rub the sanded finish with a mild abrasive, fine steel wool and a cream polish (FIG. 11-18), pumice stone and water, or rubbing compound. See Chapter 13 for rubbing instructions.

**11-18** Rub the final coat of finish with 4/0 steel wool and a cream cleaning polish.

# Chapter 12
# Antique care and identification

When an old table or chair is brought into the shop, I am usually asked, "How old is it?" and "Is it an antique?" These are not always easy questions to answer.

*Antique furniture* is generally considered to be 100 years old or older. Unique or desirable pieces less than 100 years old are considered to be *collectibles*. For tax purposes, the U.S. Customs defines an antique as an item 100 years old and not subject to import duty. Today we see an increasing number of inexpensively made oak pieces that were made in the early half of the nineteen hundreds that are being sold as antiques. These pieces can often be seen in early mail order catalogs.

"Buyer beware" is good advice for beginning collectors. Some antique shops are selling collectibles as antiques. Antique shops can also misrepresent the age of authentic antiques either by design or through ignorance. Skilled craftsmen can make new furniture look like antiques through distressing and by simulating dents, scratches, and worn areas. During the past 200 years, thousands of antique reproductions have been made. Most original antique furniture pieces are in private collections or museums.

The beginning collector should read antique magazines and books. Visits to museums and reputable antique shops are also helpful. Such exposure should help you identify features that differentiate between many furniture periods. Through knowledge of early furniture construction methods, dimensions of the item, and signs of wear, you will have more confidence that the items you purchase are authentic.

## RESTORATION

Each antique should be examined to determine if it has been damaged, altered, or if any pieces are missing. Then the rarity is determined: is it a common item or a historical museum piece? When these questions are answered, you must then decide what restoration steps should be attempted. When following proper antique refinishing procedures, common pieces can be refinished at home without damaging the patina, the aging of wood and finishes, or the value.

Once the piece has been examined, you must then decide how it will be used. Will it be a functional piece of furniture that will be used daily, or will it be a decoration? If the piece is museum quality, will restoring it lower its value as a historical document? Is the piece worth the cost of restoration? If it has been altered or if too many parts are missing, it might be better to look for something intact and in better condition.

Museum-quality furniture should be restored by a professional conservator. A fine old antique can easily be ruined by excessive modification and restoration. Removing the finish, sawing, scraping, and sanding are a few ways finishers can ruin a fine antique. Museum-quality objects should be refinished if the finish is badly damaged by excessive fire or water, if the surface has been covered with paint, or if the original finish is flaking off or missing.

If your antique is not museum quality and it is to be used at home, don't be afraid to refinish it. Throughout the text you will find references to proper methods for refinishing common antique pieces, so they can be used and enjoyed in your home.

When restoring a piece, don't overdo it. Only repair or replace parts that are necessary. Try not to alter the original piece. Use materials that can be undone if a mistake is made. Try to use similar wood parts. If the piece is made of walnut, replace damaged parts with similar walnut wood. Keep a record of what you have done by photographing the piece before, during, and after refinishing. Most important, do not destroy the patina by scraping and oversanding the wood. Dents, scratches, and burns are antique marks and should be preserved. By removing the antique marks, the value of the antique is lowered.

## CLEANING MUSEUM-QUALITY FURNITURE

Listed below are steps used by professional conservators to clean and protect historical furniture. These steps are not difficult and, with care, can be followed by home finishers.

1. To clean dust and loose dirt from the surface, vacuum with a soft brush attachment (FIG. 12-1). To prevent loose veneer from being sucked into the vacuum cleaner, lay a window screen over the surface. Tape the edges of the screen down, being careful not to apply tape to loose veneer or the veneer will peel off with the tape (FIG. 12-2).
2. To test the finish, wet a Q-Tip with water and clean a small area, picking up dirt without softening or turning the finish white (FIG. 12-3). Old shellac finishes can absorb moisture and whiten. If the finish does soften or turn white, do not use water as a cleaner; rather, clean the surface with paste wax. Apply wax to a soft cotton cloth and clean with a circular motion until no more grime can be removed, then buff.

**12-1** Vacuum sound surfaces with a soft brush attachment.

3. If the water test does not soften or turn the finish white, continue cleaning with water. Wet a sponge with water, squeeze out the water until almost dry and continue cleaning small areas, drying cleaned areas as you move on (FIG. 12-4).

4. Repeat this cleaning method using clean water and, again, thoroughly dry the finish.

5. If the piece is still dirty, add 1 teaspoon of detergent to 1 gallon of water and clean again. Finish by completely rinsing away the remaining detergent, then dry the finish. When the finish is clean, wax the piece with a paste wax.

6. If the finish is still not clean or has oil or wax on it, another cleaning method can be tried. To test the finish, wet a Q-Tip with paint thinner and clean a small obscure area, checking to see that the

finish does not soften or turn white. When the test spot has been cleaned, wipe it dry and set it aside to dry. If the finish softens or turns white, clean the piece with paste wax.

7. If the finish is not harmed by paint thinner, continue cleaning with a cloth dampened with paint thinner. Dry the cleaned finish.

8. Another more aggressive cleaning technique is to use a 4/0 steel wool pad wet with paint thinner and gently clean, moving the wet pad across the finish following the grain of the wood. When using this method be careful not to soften the finish. You must stop frequently to test the finish. The grime you are removing might actually be the finish.

**12-2** Tape a window screen over peeling veneer before vacuuming.

*Cleaning museum-quality furniture* **133**

9. Instead of painting on a new finish, it would be safer to protect the cleaned finish by applying a coat of paste wax (FIG. 12-5). Later the wax can be removed without harming the old finish. Antique conservators recommend using a microcrystalline wax (Renaissance), available from TALAS, 104 Fifth Avenue, New York, NY 10011. Paste wax application is outlined in Chapter 14.

**12-3** To test the finish, clean a small area with water and a Q-tip.

**12-4** If water does not soften or turn the finish white, continue cleaning with a wet sponge.

Do not use penetrating resin finishes over antique finishes, such as linseed oil, tung oil, penetrating resin sealers, or treatments that contain linseed oil. These finishes eventually darken and harden, and will damage the old finish when they are removed. For further information on cleaning and restoring museum-quality furniture, refer to the Bibliography—Robert F. McGiffin, *Basic Furniture Care*, New York State Office of Parks and Recreation, 1980.

Protecting antique furniture either before or after restoration is also important to its good health. Avoid sunlight, extreme temperature changes, and low or high humidity. Museums keep their relative humidity between 45 percent and 60 percent and the temperature between 65 degrees to 70 degrees F. Avoid direct sunlight; choose diffused light instead. Place ultraviolet filtering sleeves over ultraviolet-emitting fluorescent tubes. Incandescent light bulbs can be safely used.

## IDENTIFYING ANTIQUES

The first thing you will see when looking at an antique is its *patina*, the wear it is subjected to over many years of daily use. Patina can be described as the old look finishes have acquired over the years, an accumulation of dirt and wear from use and cleaning. There are scratches and cracks in the finish, along with dents, burns, and splits. Old finishes become darker and richer in color. Unfinished wood can turn from a amber yellow to light brown.

**12-5** When the piece is clean, apply a coat of paste wax.

### Signs of wear

- Edges are rounded and dented on tabletops and chairs.
- The edges of carvings are dulled.
- Wood shrinks against the grain and warps.
- The bottom of legs on tables and chairs are worn and dented from bumping and cleaning.
- Front rungs on chairs and tables are worn on their top sides by shoes rubbing on them.
- The bottom sides of drawers are worn down from years of opening and closing.

### Builder's marks

Look for lathe grooves cut into the turned rungs on chair, table, and bed posts. Early lathes were turned slowly by hand. The cutting tools left faint rings in these parts. No two identical turned parts will be exactly alike.

Two-man hand saws were used to cut boards used in cabinet construction. Look for straight saw marks on boards used on the back of cabinets, inside drawers, and other construction pieces. Circular saws were in general use after 1850 and left circular or curved saw marks on the wood.

Awls were used as pencils. Workmen scratched patterns in the wood where holes were to be chiseled out for hinges, legs, locks, and dovetail joints on drawers.

Roman numerals were used on the underside of sets of chairs and on poster beds to mark the position of the pieces. The numbers were cut into the wood with a small chisel.

Craftsmen used jack planes to smooth rough lumber. The planes had curved blades that left small concave grooves in the wood. These marks can be found on the bottom of drawers and the wood on the backs and inside of cabinets.

When refinishing, do not sand or scrape away these marks of age!

## Materials

Early handmade screws, crudely made with blunt tips and off-center slots, were made before 1800. Machine-made screws were made after 1850.

Hand-forged, square-head nails, rough and irregular with hammered heads, were in use before 1800 and were still in use as late as 1870. Smooth, machine-cut, square-head nails were in use from 1800 to 1890. After 1890, modern wire cut nails were introduced. Square nails are still being made and used.

Dovetail joints with flared tenons, the projecting part cut into the end of a piece of wood that is to be inserted into a corresponding hole, were used to join the side of drawers to the drawer fronts. They can give an approximate date to a piece. Wide one-piece tenons were used in the seventeenth century. Multiple, irregular, hand-cut tenons were made in the eighteenth century. Uniform machine-cut tenons were used after 1800.

Drawer handles were often attached with split pins prior to 1750. After 1750, a nut and bolt fastening was used to attach handles.

These dates are approximate. It is not always possible to set exact times when special construction methods or materials were used. Because of culture lag, one factory or shop could be using new construction methods and materials, while an adjacent shop could be using older techniques and materials.

# Chapter 13

# Hand-rubbed finishes

When a fine piece of furniture is being described, it is often said that it has a hand-rubbed finish. Hand-rubbed finishes and fine furniture go together. Factory-finished furniture might not be hand-rubbed. Some factory-finished pieces are coated with a flat finish that requires no rubbing. Other factory pieces are sprayed with semigloss or gloss coatings. These finishes are machine rubbed, but on expensive furniture they are hand rubbed.

Rubbing the final coat of finish after it dries is an important step in the finishing process. Varnish and urethane coatings that are brushed at home are usually not rubbed. This step is where we separate the amateur from the experienced finisher. Beginning finishers often miss this important step. Home-brushed finishes should be rubbed. Rubbing eliminates these small imperfections like dirt spots and brush lines, making the surface smooth and giving the finish any luster you wish.

Sprayed finishes also need rubbing. Lacquer and urethane finishes that have been sprayed can have dust embedded in the finish, or there might be rough spots and runs. The surface might be covered with *orange peel*, small bumps on the surface similar to the bumps on an orange. Fortunately, these problems can be corrected by rubbing. A brushed or sprayed finish properly rubbed can look as good or better than factory-finished furniture. Figure 13-1 pictures several different rubbing materials.

## FINISHES AND RUBBING

When a finish is rubbed with an abrasive, the finish is slowly worn away, high spots are leveled, dirt and rough spots are rubbed off, and a smooth surface is obtained. Small scratches from the rubbing abrasive are left on the finish. If these fine scratches are uniform and follow the grain of the wood, they look natural and improve the beauty of the finish.

**13-1** Rubbing materials used to hand rub finishes: rubbing compound, pumice stone, rottenstone, and steel wool.

Light striking a rough surface, one that has been rubbed with a course abrasive or coated with a flat finish, is refracted or defused. Light from this surface is not reflected directly back to your eyes, and the surface appears dull. Scratching or roughing a finish causes it to dull.

Light striking a smooth surface, a surface that has been rubbed with a fine abrasive or coated with a gloss finish, is reflected back to your eyes. You see a bright, glossy finish. Smoothing and polishing a surface makes it shiny.

If the finish is rubbed across the grain, ugly scratches that are difficult to remove appear, requiring extra rubbing to remove them. Always rub in the direction of the grain, never across the grain.

### Flat finishes

Finishes that dry dull with no shine are called *flat, dull, dead flat*, or *matt*. These finishes are seen on Danish modern furniture. Finishes that dry flat can be an oil-type finish, linseed oil, tung oil, or penetrating sealer. Lacquer, varnish, and urethane finishes that have had a flattening material added to them also dry flat.

### Satin finishes

Satin or semigloss finishes dry dull, but not as dull as flat finishes. Semigloss is a better way to describe them, somewhere between a flat and a gloss. Satin is probably the best all-around sheen to use.

After a satin finish has been applied, if the finish is smooth and clean with no objectionable imperfections, rubbing is not necessary. If the finish is dirty or you do not like the sheen, it can be rubbed to further dull it or to bring out more gloss.

Flat and satin finishes hide imperfections. They also tend to be hazy and obscure the wood if several coats are applied. When more than two coats of flat varnish or urethane are to be used, make the first coats gloss; then add a final coat of flat or satin over the gloss.

### Gloss finishes

Gloss finishes dry with a bright, shiny luster. They glaringly show every imperfection in the finish—dust spots, runs, and brush lines. Rubbing is a must to remove these blemishes and give the finish a smooth high-gloss surface.

### Varnish and lacquer finishes

Varnish and lacquer finishes are easy to rub. They can be made to look soft and mellow or bright and shiny.

### Urethane

Urethane can also be rubbed, but unlike varnish and lacquer, it is hard to rub. This finish has a tough surface that is difficult to cut with rubbing abrasive. A rubbed urethane surface does not look as soft and fine as rubbed varnish or lacquer.

### Oil finishes

Penetrating sealers, tung oil, and linseed oil finishes dry dull. They only need a light rubbing with fine steel wool.

## SANDING FINISHES PRIOR TO RUBBING

Before rubbing a finish, sand the surface smooth. Sanding the finish will remove dust spots, brush marks, and runs.

After a generous amount of finish has been applied and allowed to dry hard, sand varnish and urethane finishes with 400-grit wet or dry sandpaper, water, and a sanding block. Thoroughly wet the paper and surface with water; on lacquer, use paint thinner. Lightly and evenly sand the finish (FIG. 13-2). Water keeps the sandpaper from becoming clogged with sanded finish, allowing the paper to move smoothly across the surface. If the finish is lacquer, water will work, but paint thinner works better.

Sandpaper first cuts off high spots; they will look dull. The shiny spots are low areas in the finish. As you sand, and more finish is sanded away, the dull areas will increase. Ideally, a perfectly smooth surface will be completely dull with no shiny spots. This is difficult to obtain. There is always the chance of sanding through the finish into the wood.

**13-2** Lightly sand the finish on a flat surface before rubbing.

If you do sand through to the surface, restain the spot and apply another coat of finish. It takes experience to know when to stop sanding or rubbing before going through. Do not attempt to sand round surfaces with sandpaper. Instead, lightly rub them with 4/0 steel wool.

When the surface has been smoothed with sandpaper, go on to the next step—rubbing the sanded finish with steel wool or pumice stone. For your first project, to avoid sanding or rubbing through, forego the sandpaper and use steel wool as your rubbing abrasive. Steel wool is the safest abrasive to use. It burnishes the finish, rolls over high spots without cutting them down, and lessens the chance of rubbing through the finish.

## FLAT FINISH USING STEEL WOOL

To obtain a hand-rubbed flat finish, coat the wood with a flat or satin finish. It can be lacquer, varnish, or urethane. A gloss finish can also be rubbed to make it dull. When a generous amount of finish has been applied and dried, carefully sand level surfaces with 400-grit wet or dry sandpaper. Sanding is an optional step and can be skipped if you think that you might sand through.

When sanded, or if you choose not to sand, rub the finish with 3/0 steel wool that has been dipped in 4/F (fine) pumice stone and water. Rub evenly with the grain; use short strokes. Finish off by rubbing with long strokes all the way across the surface. Rub up to the edges but not over them. Rubbing abrasive will quickly cut through the edges.

After the surface is rubbed with pumice, completely wipe off any residual pumice with a damp cloth and dry. Use cream polish to brighten the finish if it is too dull.

*Materials*

Flat or satin finish (lacquer, varnish, or urethane)

400-grit wet or dry sandpaper

Sandpaper block

3/0 steel wool

4/F pumice stone and water

Soft rags

*Application*

1. Apply a flat finish (heavy).
2. Carefully level dust spots on flat surfaces with 400-grit sandpaper. Use a sandpaper block and water as a lubricant.
3. Rub the finish with 3/0 steel wool that has been dipped in 4/F pumice stone and water.
4. Remove pumice with a soft wet rag and dry.
5. Polish with a cream polish for more gloss.

## SEMIGLOSS FINISH USING STEEL WOOL

For a semigloss finish, sand the surface with 400-grit wet or dry sandpaper; then rub with 4/0 steel wool that is wet with cream furniture polish (FIG. 13-3). Cream polish helps the steel wool move smoothly across the surface with less dulling. When the finish is rubbed, buff off excess polish for a smooth semigloss finish. If the finish is too shiny, lightly rub with a dry 4/0 steel wool pad until the finish has the proper sheen.

*Materials*

Flat or satin finish

400-grit wet or dry sandpaper

Sandpaper block

4/0 steel wool

Cream furniture polish

Soft rags

*Application*

1. Apply a flat or satin finish (heavy).
2. Carefully level out spots on flat surfaces with 400-grit sandpaper. Use a sandpaper block and water as a lubricant.
3. Rub the finish with 4/0 steel wool that has been dipped in cream polish.
4. Wipe the piece dry with a soft rag.

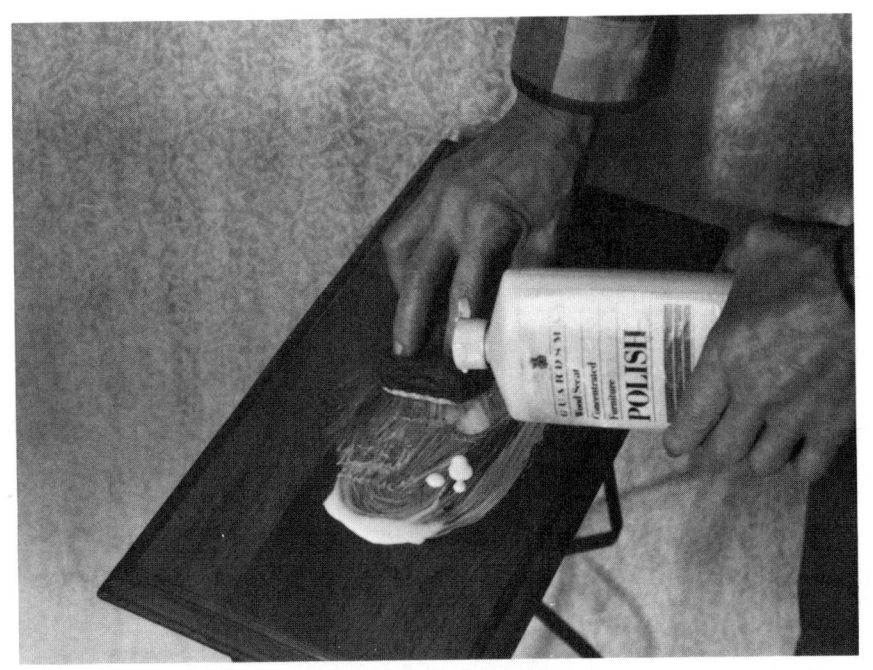

**13-3** For a semigloss finish, rub with steel wool and a cream cleaning polish.

## SEMIGLOSS FINISH USING PUMICE STONE

Another way to obtain a semigloss surface is to rub the finish with a rubbing pad and pumice stone. Furniture finishers use pumice to rub their finishes. This is where we separate the amateur from the professional. The beginner will either not rub the project or will only use steel wool. This is fine; even better, it is safe. There is less chance of rubbing through with steel wool. The experienced finisher will forego the use of steel wool and rub with pumice.

Rubbing with pumice stone will give the finish a smooth, good-looking satin or semigloss sheen. This finish is my favorite—not too dull to be dead or too glossy to show every imperfection. Before rubbing with pumice, a word of caution. Pumice actually cuts the finish and wears it away. If there is not a heavy coat of finish on the surface, you can easily rub through to the wood. It takes practice and experience to know when to stop.

### Rubbing

Apply a heavy coat of finish. When dry, sand level surfaces with 400-grit wet or dry sandpaper. Fold a soft cloth into a square pad that is slightly larger than your hand and several layers thick. The bottom of the pad must be flat and smooth, with no wrinkles, folds, or buttons. A blackboard eraser or a felt rubbing block may be used.

Soak the pad and wet the surface with water. Sprinkle 4/F (fine) pumice stone from the container or, if dirty, pour into a nylon stocking and shake onto the finish. The pumice must be clean. Any dirt in the pumice will leave scratches in the finish that will be difficult to rub out.

Lay the wet rubbing pad on the pumice and rub evenly with short 12-inch strokes. Apply mild, even pressure; do not bear down with all your strength; rub evenly with the grain. On flat surfaces, avoid rubbing over the edges because it is easy to rub through (FIG. 13-4).

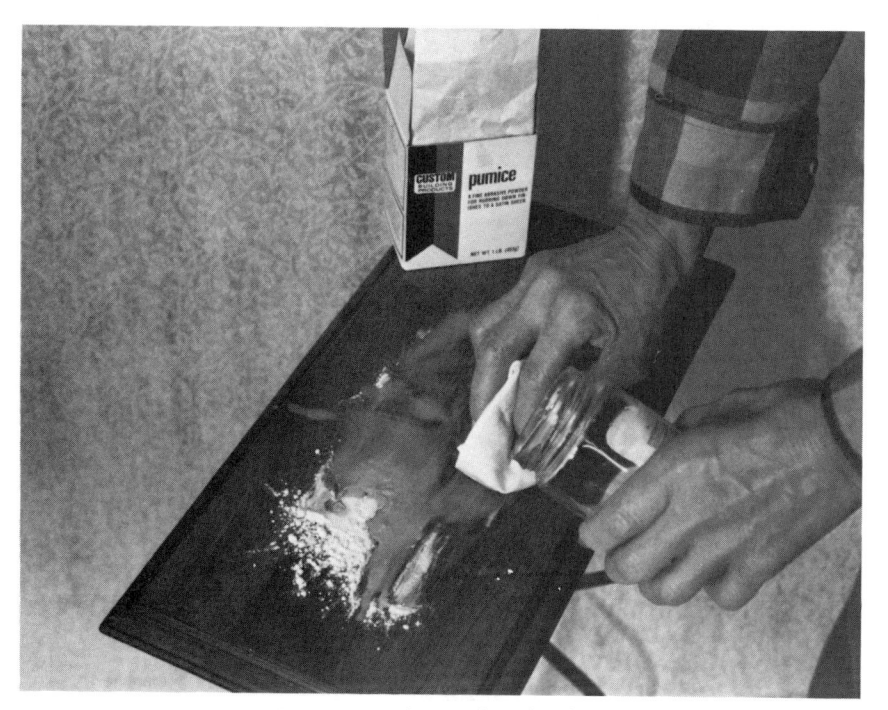

**13-4** Use a soft cloth, pumice stone, and water for a hand-rubbed semigloss surface.

After rubbing the surface evenly with short strokes, finish off by rubbing with long strokes all the way across the surface. Add water to the pad when it becomes dry; it must move easily across the surface without dragging. Too much water will wash pumice away; not enough water will cause the pad to drag.

When the finish has been rubbed evenly, remove all traces of pumice that is on the surface with a damp rag. Dry with a soft, clean cloth. Look at the finish under a good light. The project should be between the light and your eyes. If the finish is smooth and has a uniform sheen, you are finished; if not, apply more pumice and rub until the sheen is uniform.

*Materials*

Flat or satin finish—lacquer, varnish, or urethane

400-grit wet or dry sandpaper

Sandpaper block

4/F pumice stone and water

Rags

*Application*

1. Apply a flat or satin finish (heavy).
2. Carefully level dust spots on flat surfaces with 400-grit sandpaper. Use a sandpaper block and water as a lubricant.
3. Rub the sanded surface with a cloth pad that has been dipped in 4/F pumice stone and water.
4. When the rubbing has been completed, remove all traces of pumice with a wet rag.
5. To brighten, polish with a cream polish.

## Oil and pumice

Instead of mixing water with pumice, the old-time finishers used a mixture of white gasoline and paraffin oil. Mixed with pumice, this mixture gives a satin-smooth surface. The problem is gasoline is dangerous and paraffin oil is messy and coats hands, clothes, and furniture. Water as a lubricant is easier to use without the danger of gasoline or the mess of paraffin oil.

## GLOSS FINISH HAND-RUBBED WITH ROTTENSTONE

If you prefer a gloss finish, begin by applying a gloss finish. It can be varnish, urethane, lacquer, or any on-surface gloss finish.

When a generous amount of finish has been applied and thoroughly dried, lightly sand flat surfaces with water and 400-grit sandpaper. Next, rub the surface with pumice stone and water. After the finish has been rubbed smooth, clean off all remaining pumice.

Prepare a new rubbing pad and rub the surface with rottenstone (FIG. 13-5). Follow the same steps as outlined for rubbing with pumice stone. Doesn't sound very appetizing does it? Rottenstone is a siliceous limestone. When the rock is first crushed, it gives off an unpleasant odor. Fortunately, when you use it, the odor is gone. Rottenstone is crushed to a very-fine powdery abrasive. When a finish is rubbed with this abrasive, it takes on a beautiful glossy sheen.

If you are unable to find rottenstone at your paint or hardware store, use an extra-fine automobile rubbing compound in its place. Most auto supply stores stock automobile rubbing compound.

*Materials*

Gloss finish—lacquer, varnish, or urethane

400-grit wet or dry sandpaper

Sandpaper block

4/F pumice stone and water

Rottenstone or fine automotive rubbing compound

Soft rags

*Application*

1. Apply a gloss finish.
2. Carefully level dust spots on flat surfaces with 400-grit sandpaper. Use a sandpaper block and water as a lubricant.
3. Rub the sanded surface with a cloth pad that has been dipped in 4/F pumice stone and water.
4. When the surface has been rubbed smooth, remove all traces of pumice with a wet rag.
5. Prepare a second rubbing pad and rub with rottenstone and water or a fine automotive rubbing compound.
6. For an extra-bright surface, before polishing or waxing, buff the rubbed surface with an electric buffer that has a clean sheepskin bonnet attached.
7. Polish with a cream polish or wax with a hard paste wax.

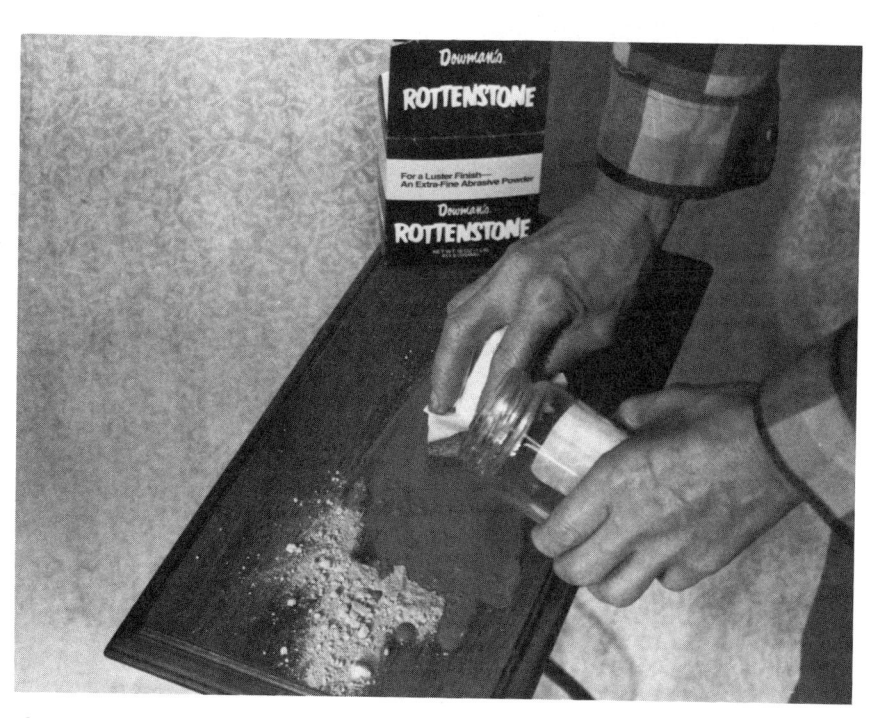

**13-5** For a high-gloss surface, rub with rottenstone and water.

## ELECTRIC BUFFER FOR A HIGH-GLOSS FINISH

For an extra high-gloss finish, buff the hand-rubbed surface with an electric polisher that has a sheepskin bonnet attached to it. When you finish hand rubbing the surface, leave a trace of the rubbing material behind. It will help the buffer polish the finish smoother and faster. If you rubbed with an automotive or furniture rubbing compound, do not buff it unless the compound is made to be used with an electric buffer; not all rubbing compounds are. Some hand-rubbing compounds contain wax that will gum up on buffer pads.

To use the buffer, hold it tightly in both hands. Turn it on and whisk it across the finish. Hold the machine level as it is moved; tilting can cause the pad to burn the finish. Until you become experienced, do not bear down hard. The weight of the buffer is often all the pressure that is needed (FIG. 13-6).

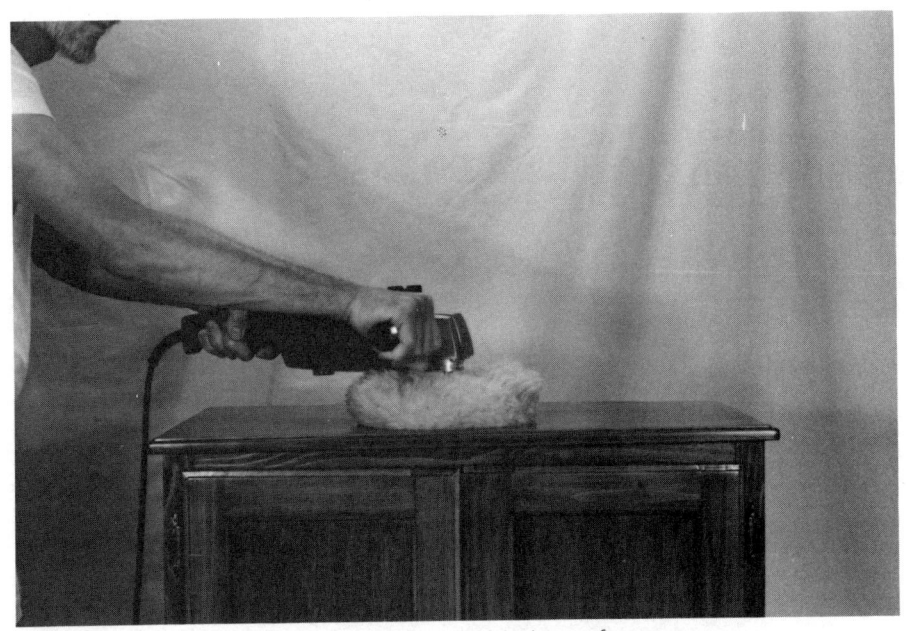

**13-6** Use an electric buffer to produce an extra-high-gloss surface.

On lightweight machines, pressing hard can cause the pad to turn too slowly. On machines that turn at a high rpm, extra pressure can make the machine burn the finish, softening and pulling it away from the wood. Because edges are easy to burn through, buff up to the edges but not over them.

If the buffer pad becomes dirty because finish becomes embedded in the pad, clean or replace it. A dirty pad can burn or leave circular streaks in the finish. To clean the buffer pad, comb it with a wire brush and wash it in soap and water. Attach the wet pad to the buffer and spin dry.

## RUBBING LEGS AND TURNINGS

*Turnings*, the round spindles and stretchers on chairs and tables, should be rubbed. Extra care must be given to flutes, carvings, and bulbs on turnings. Never use sandpaper on turnings or rub too long or hard on one spot.

For a flat finish, rub the turnings with a moistened 3/0 steel wool pad and 4/F (fine) pumice stone. Wet the steel wool in water.

For a semigloss finish, rub with 3/0 steel wool that has been soaked in cream polish (FIG. 13-7).

For a gloss finish, rub with 4/0 steel wool and cream polish. Next, rub with a soft cloth that is wet with water and rottenstone. You can substitute a fine rubbing compound in place of rottenstone. When you finish the rubbing, clean off all abrasive and polish with a hard paste wax to give the finish an extra-high luster.

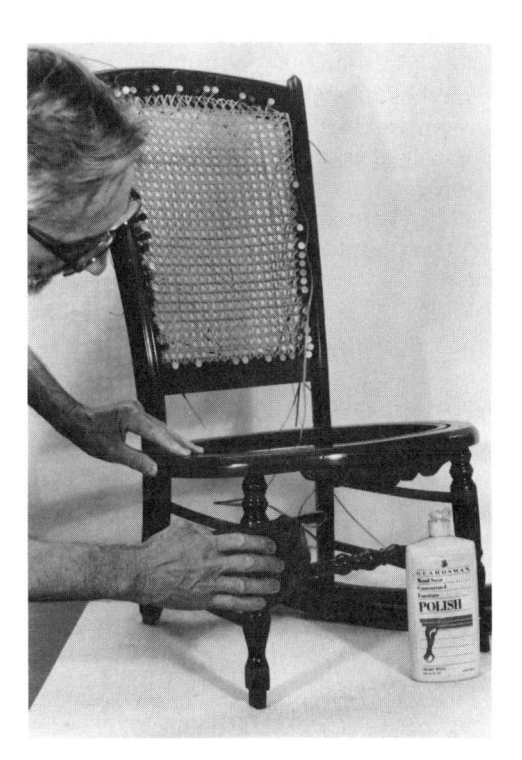

**13-7** Rub turnings with steel wool and cream polish.

# Chapter 14

# Polishing

Advertisers in magazines and on television are forever extolling their furniture polishes, telling us how they are easy to use and require no buffing or rubbing—instant magic. Unfortunately, many of these polishes can cause more problems than shine, maybe instant trouble. The easy-to-apply polishes often contain soft waxes that are easy to apply but not long lasting. After a few applications the surface can become soft and sticky.

Silicone polishes are easy to apply and give a high luster. After repeated applications, however, the silicones penetrate through the finish, filling the wood and backing up onto the surface, leaving a silicone buildup. This buildup is hard to remove, making cleaning and refinishing more difficult.

## WIPING OUT ADVERTISEMENTS AND MYTHS

Most furniture manufacturers recommend that their new furniture be dusted with a damp cloth or cleaned with a mild detergent. They do not want gooey polishes smeared on the furniture they make.

Proper waxing, if you must wax, should be done with a hard paste wax, preferably one containing carnauba wax, the hardest wax available. One coat of wax can last from six months to one year and needs only an occasional dusting with a damp cloth. To remove excess dirt and oil from an on-the-surface finish or waxed surface, clean with a cream cleaning polish.

When you visit a supermarket and view the rows of polishes that are prominently displayed, you might be bewildered to know which polish or wax to choose. There are many different types of polishing products and manufacturers, each promising miracles. Unfortunately, some have the potential to cause problems and to actually damage a finish.

The following polishes are divided into three groups: oils, waxes, and cleaning polishes (FIG. 14-1). Their good and bad points are discussed, with some suggestions on how to use them.

**14-1** Left to right: a penetrating oil finish polish, oil polish, waxes, and cream cleaning polish.

## OIL POLISHES

Oil polishes are made from the same oils that are taken from the ground, refined, and used in an automobile. Any of these oils—10-weight engine oil, three-in-one oil, and mineral oil—could be used to make an oil polish. Thinners, fragrances, and colors are added to make them look and smell better.

Oil polishes are best when used on old varnish finishes. Oils keep varnish from drying out and the finish from cracking. Oil polish is good to use on old furniture that is hazing or turning white. It can hide small scratches and can protect wood from moisture. This is the best polish to use on in-the-wood finishes. Oil polishes include linseed oil, tung oil, and penetrating oil finishes.

There are disadvantages to oil polishes, however. They often leave an oily film on the finish that collects dust, shows fingerprints, and can darken the finish. Oil polishes must be applied often to maintain a bright finish. Painted surfaces yellow if oil is repeatedly applied. Oil should not be used on lacquer finishes; most factory-finished furniture is coated with lacquer.

### White oil polish

White oil polish contains water mixed with oil that is emulsified. Water in the mixture cleans water-soluble dirt. The oil cleans oil-soluble dirt.

### Lemon oil polish

Most lemon oil polishes contain little or no lemon oil. These polishes are made with oils that are mixed with lemon scent and yellow color. Real lemon oil is an excellent cleaner, but it is expensive, and if added to polish, it is added in such small quantities that it has little effect.

### Scratch-removing oil

Scratch-removing oil is an oil polish with stain color added. When applied to a damaged finish, dents and scratches are temporarily darkened by the color in the polish. Oil polishes are easy to apply; wipe them on with a rag and wipe off. They brighten the finish for a short time but soon turn dull, requiring frequent applications.

## WAX POLISHES

Paste wax can protect a finish. It shields the finish from water and minor abrasions, giving the surface a bright luster.

The best waxes contain carnauba or candelilla wax, the hardest waxes used in paste wax. Soft waxes containing beeswax and paraffin wax offer less protection. If a hard furniture paste wax cannot be found, use a hard automobile paste wax; it works as well.

Wax resists scuffing, spilled water, and alcohol. Wax is harder to apply than an oil polish, but it is only necessary to use it once or twice a year.

One coat of wax is all that is needed to protect the finish. When a new coat of wax is applied, the old wax should be removed. Applying successive layers of wax without cleaning off preceding coats will cause a wax buildup, embedding dirt and grime under each wax layer.

### Removing a wax buildup

After successive coats of wax are applied to a finish, it will begin to turn yellow, become sticky, and be difficult to buff to a shine. To remove a wax buildup, or to remove old wax prior to waxing, wash the surface with a cloth dampened with paint thinner. When the surface is clean and dry, apply a new coat of wax.

Paint thinner will remove wax, but it will not take off a silicone buildup. See silicone removal later in this chapter.

### Paste wax application

To apply a hard paste wax, first remove the old wax with paint thinner. When the surface is clean and dry, pick up a small amount of wax from the can with a soft cloth that has been dampened with water. Rub the wax on one small area. If too large an area is waxed at one time, the wax might harden before it can be buffed out. With another soft clean rag, lightly rub over and smooth out the wax. Allow it to set for two or three minutes. Before it dries hard, buff with a smooth, soft cloth; cotton diapers are excellent. Rub the wax in a circular motion; then finish by rubbing with the grain.

To make buffing easier, instead of dampening the wax applicator cloth with water, slightly wet it with paint thinner. Paste wax lightly thinned with paint thinner will lay on the finish smoother and thinner, making buffing easier.

Once the piece has been waxed, all that is needed is an occasional dusting with a damp cloth or brightening with a cream cleaning polish. Unless the piece receives excessive use, three months between cleanings with a cream polish is adequate. Avoid using aerosols or polishes containing silicones.

Paste wax is harder to apply than an oil polish, but it is only used once or twice a year, and it does protect the finish. Oil polishes must be applied repeatedly and gives little protection.

Excessive waxing can cause a wax buildup. Old wax must be removed from the finish before rewaxing.

Hard paste waxes dry with a high gloss and should not be used over penetrating oil finishes, linseed oil, tung oil, or penetrating sealers. The sheen on these finishes is flat; gloss wax will cause them to shine. Wax will yellow painted surfaces.

### Scratch-removing paste wax

Wax with dark color added can be used to hide light spots caused by dents and scratches. Color in the wax penetrates into the light spots, darkening them. If a commercially darkened wax polish is not available, use brown or cordovan shoe polish to hide light-colored nicks and scratches on walnut and mahogany finishes.

### Flat wax

Beeswax and paraffin wax dry with little shine. To make your own, melt equal parts of beeswax and paraffin wax together. This polish is good for low-luster finishes.

## CREAM CLEANING POLISHES

Cream cleaning polishes remove dirt and grime from finishes without leaving a heavy wax or oily film. If cleaning polishes are used properly, there is no wax buildup or wax haze. They dry to a pleasant satin sheen and will not yellow painted surfaces.

For routine care of finishes, cleaning polishes are excellent. Wipe them on and buff dry with a soft cloth. They can be used to clean lacquer, varnish, and urethane finishes, or to clean finishes that have been waxed. Use them sparingly unless the surface is exposed to excessive use. Three months between cleanings is adequate.

## SILICONE POLISHES

Liquid and aerosol polishes that contain silicones can damage finishes. They should be used sparingly on fine wood finishes.

Silicones can leave a white deposit in pores that cannot be cleaned out. They can cause a wax buildup that is almost impossible to remove, making refinishing difficult.

Silicone is finely ground quartz in liquid form. When added to polish, silicones give a durable high-gloss sheen desired by polish manufacturers. Unfortunately, silicones in the polish penetrate through the finish, soak into the wood, and eventually back up onto the surface of the finish, causing a silicone buildup. Veneer and parquet tabletops will loosen and peel quicker when exposed to water if silicone polishes have been used on them. Silicone tends to increase water damage.

Many liquid polishes and aerosol spray polishes contain silicones. Reading the product's label does not help; few manufacturers list silicones on the container.

### Removing a silicone buildup

To remove a silicone wax buildup from a finish, try washing it off with benzine. If this fails, wash the surface with ammonia detergent that has been mixed 50–50 with water. Do not leave it on too long. Ammonia can scar the finish. If these methods fail, rub the finish with water and furniture or automotive rubbing compound. It takes lots of rubbing, but it does work. When the silicone has been removed, go over the finish with a cream cleaning polish, or apply a paste wax if the cleaned finish is too dull.

### Finishing over silicone

Once a polish containing silicone is used on a finish, the silicone can never be removed. It is in the finish. Remove the finish and it is still in the wood. You can try to clean it off the wood with lacquer thinner or benzine, but no matter how hard the surface is scrubbed or sanded, the silicone can never be completely removed.

When a new finish is applied over an existing finish, or wood that has silicone in it, small pinholes appear. These holes spread and become large holes in the finish. Finishers call them *fish eyes*. A special silicone additive must be mixed with the finish to help it flow out and cover the holes. See the information on spray problems causing fish eyes in Chapter 10.

To test a surface for silicone, rub your fingers across the finish. If the surface is slippery, and your fingertips pick up a slick waxy coating, there might be silicone on it. Another test is to pour paint thinner on the finish. If it is coated with silicone, the paint thinner will bead up and pull away from the surface, forming small round holes that resemble fish eyes.

## PAINTED SURFACES

Painted furniture and woodwork require special care. Wax and oil polish will turn them yellow. Clean away water-soluble dirt with water and a mild detergent. Remove oil-soluble grime with paint thinner. To polish, occasionally clean with a cream cleaning polish.

# Chapter 15

# Touching up

*M*aking touch-up repairs is an important part of finishing. Many finishers do nothing but touch-up work. Finishers are employed by furniture stores to repair damaged furniture or to make house calls, making the repairs in the home. They repair nicks, scratches, rub marks, and small breaks.

The purpose of touching up is to make repairs to damaged furniture without refinishing the article. The finisher first uses his touch-up medicines. If these fail, the finish must be removed, which increases the cost, time, and the possibility that the finish might not match perfectly. There are many furniture factories, each with its own special finishes and finishing methods. It takes considerable skill and sometimes luck to match every finish. You don't want to be forced to remove a good finish.

When making touch-up repairs, it is important that you do not cause more damage to the finish, such as burning or blistering the finish when burning-in; using the wrong colors with a touch up; or sanding or rubbing through the finish.

## SIMPLE REPAIRS YOU CAN MAKE

If your furniture becomes damaged or stained, refer to this guide for proper treatment. If the damage is extensive, consult a professional furniture finisher.

### Alcohol damage

Perfumes, medicines, beverages, and other liquids containing alcohol can quickly dissolve many finishes. Immediately blot up spills. If damage has occurred, try lightly rubbing the spot with a cloth dampened with ammonia; the rag should be almost dry. Then polish with a paste wax.

Oil finishes can be sanded and reoiled with an oil finish or penetrating sealer.

## Block spots

Black spots on wood are caused by water. Water has penetrated through the finish, soaking into and darkening the wood.

To repair, remove the finish, sand the wood, and bleach the black spot with a saturate solution of oxalic acid. On softwood (pine and fir), the black spots disappear quickly. On hardwood (maple and oak), it takes longer for the spot to disappear. The wood must be kept wet with oxalic acid for one hour or more. When the black spots disappear, spread the remaining acid over the surface. After a few minutes, remove the acid with water and dry, then neutralize the surface with vinegar. When dry, sand and refinish the surface (see Chapter 6, *Bleaching*).

## Candle wax

Gently scrape off chunks of wax with your fingernail or a plastic scraper. Wipe with a cloth wet with paint thinner to remove remaining wax. An ice cube placed over the wax will harden it, making scraping easier. Place a heavy blotter over the wax spill and heat with a warm iron. The softened wax will be absorbed by the blotter.

## Cigarette burns

If the burn is on top of the finish, try rubbing it away with steel wool and cream polish, fine pumice stone and water, or rubbing compound. If this resolves the problem, wax the surface. Unfortunately, most burns go through the finish, charring the wood. When this occurs, the charred wood must be scraped away, filled with putty or burn-in material, and if necessary, grained to match the surrounding grain pattern and coated with finish.

## Hot spots

White spots on the finish that are caused by heat can be difficult to remove. The surface might need to be recoated with finish. If the finish is not badly damaged, rubbing the spot with oil and an abrasive might remove it. See how to remove white spots in "*Water Damage*" later in this chapter.

## Nail polish

If the nail polish has not penetrated the finish and is wet, blot it up. When the remaining nail polish hardens, sand level with 400-grit sandpaper, a sandpaper block, and paint thinner. Finish by rubbing the surface with 4/0 steel wool and a cream cleaning polish, fine pumice stone and water, or rubbing compound.

If the polish hardens before it can be blotted, scrape it off with a single-edge razor blade. Try not to scratch the finish. Sand away the remaining fingernail polish with 400-grit sandpaper, paint thinner, and a sandpaper block. Finish by rubbing with 4/0 steel wool and cream polish, fine pumice stone and water, or rubbing compound.

### Paint

Use paint thinner to remove fresh oil-base paints. Use water to remove fresh latex paints.

Soak hardened oil-base paints with linseed oil. Allow it to stand until the paint softens. Hardened latex paint must be scraped or sanded off. Once hardened latex will not soften in water.

### Minor scratches and dents

Small surface blemishes that are not light in color can be removed by rubbing. First try 4/0 steel wool and cream cleaning polish. If the blemishes persist, sand lightly with 400-grit sandpaper, wet with paint thinner or water. Then rub with 4/0 steel wool and cream polish, pumice and water, or rubbing compound.

Scratches that are white can be temporarily darkened by coloring with scratch-removing oil or wax. Try shoe polish; use brown for walnut and cordovan for mahogany. Iodine colors cherry; dilute it with alcohol and it makes maple.

## BURNING-IN TO REPAIR DEEP DENTS AND SCRATCHES

### Wax sticks

You can make temporary repairs to deep dents and scratches by rubbing colored crayons or commercially prepared wax sticks into the holes. Rub or melt the wax sticks into the indentations. If the wax color is not right or you are not satisfied with the repair, remove the wax with paint thinner and a cloth.

### Finishing materials

The professional way to repair shallow dents and scratches is to fill the dents with finishing material: lacquer for lacquer finishes and varnish for varnish finishes.

Fill the indentation with finish, a little higher than the surrounding surface. Dry for several days until your fingernail does not leave an impression. If the finish sinks, apply more finish. When dry, scrape off high spots with a razor blade and sand level with 400-grit sandpaper, using water for varnish or paint thinner for lacquer. Use a sandpaper block. After sanding, rub the entire surface with fine pumice stone and water, or 4/0 steel wool. If necessary, recoat the surface with finish.

### Burning-in

Another professional method of repairing deep dents and scratches is to fill the hole using a burn-in stick, also called a lacquer stick, or shellac stick. This method of repairing is called *burning-in*. A burn-in stick is similar to sealing wax; when heated it melts, when cool it hardens. Burn-in sticks come in about 100 furniture colors. Figure 15-1 shows an assortment of tools that could be used to make a burn-in.

**15-1** Tools that are used to fill holes in finishes: burn-in irons, electric heater, alcohol lamp, and burn-in sticks.

To make a burn-in, melt out a small amount of burn-in stick with a hot iron, place it in the dent, and smooth it over with the hot burn-in iron. When the burn-in material cools, it hardens, which takes about five seconds. Once hard, sand it smooth, rub it, and if necessary, coat with finish. This method of repairing is indispensable to furniture refinishers who work in furniture stores. The finisher spends most of the day burning-in and touching up (*deluxing*) so the merchandise will be in perfect condition when it is received by the customer.

The burn-in method of filling dents can be rewarding. Large dents can be filled and repaired quickly and invisibly. This method of repairing takes considerable time to learn. Practice and patience are required. A hot burn-in iron can quickly burn and blister the surrounding finish. Selection of the wrong burn-in color, or not filling the hole or smoothing the filler properly, or sanding through the finish are a few of the problems to overcome. Always practice on an unwanted finished surface before attempting to repair a valuable piece.

*Materials*

Burn-in knife

Alcohol lamp, can of sterno, or electric knife or oven

Burn-in sticks; select colors to match the finish

400-grit wet or dry sandpaper and paint thinner

Sandpaper block

Vaseline and water

Rubbing materials (4/F pumice stone or 4/0 steel wool)

A grapefruit knife makes a good burn-in iron, as does an artist's spatula (a firm but flexible blade is needed). Burn-in irons that come in different sizes and shapes can be purchased from finishing supply dealers, including electric burn-in irons with changeable tips and an electric oven that heats irons.

To heat the burn-in iron, use an alcohol lamp or a can of sterno. You need a sootless flame. A gas flame will deposit soot on the burn-in iron, causing the burn-in material to darken and discolor.

The tip of the burn-in iron must be kept clean when burning in. Dirt or baked on burn-in material on the tip will stick to and blister the area around the burn-in and pull the finish from the surface. Wipe the blade across a steel wool pad to clean it. Do this frequently as the burn-in progresses.

Apply Vaseline around the dent, not in it, to lessen the chance of burning the surrounding finish and to make removing excess filler easier. Practice on a scrap piece because you won't want to ruin your good furniture.

Use wet or dry 400-grit sandpaper, a sandpaper block, and paint thinner to sand down excess burn-in material. To blend the sanded burn-in into the surrounding finish, rub with pumice stone and water, rubbing compound, or steel wool.

### Making the burn-in

Heat the burn-in knife with a soot-free alcohol flame or use an electric burn-in iron. Wipe the blade clean with steel wool.

Remove a small amount of colored filler from the burn-in stick with the tip of the hot knife and carefully place it in the hole (FIG. 15-2). Different colored burn-in sticks can be melted together to match the finish better.

Rub a small amount of Vaseline onto the surface around the fill. With the tip of your finger place a drop of water on top of the burn-in. This water will help keep the filler from boiling and the surrounding finish from blistering if the burn-in iron is too hot.

If necessary reheat the burn-in knife. Do not make it too hot because you don't want to burn the surrounding finish. Wipe the blade clean with steel wool and lightly and quickly whisk the knife across the burn-in material, pushing it into the hole and smoothing it out flush with the surrounding surface. Move the knife rapidly, touching only the filler. Try not to touch the surrounding finish with the hot blade because the finish will easily burn and blister.

After the hole is filled and the filler smoothed out, sand the filler level with the surrounding surface. Use 400-grit wet or dry sandpaper, paint thinner for a lubricant, and a small sandpaper block (FIG. 15-3). The last step is to rub the entire surface with 4/F pumice stone and water or 4/0 steel wool and a cream polish. Figure 15-4 shows a sanded burn-in being rubbed with steel wool.

**15-2** Fill dents and scratches in finishes by melting lacquer sticks into the holes.

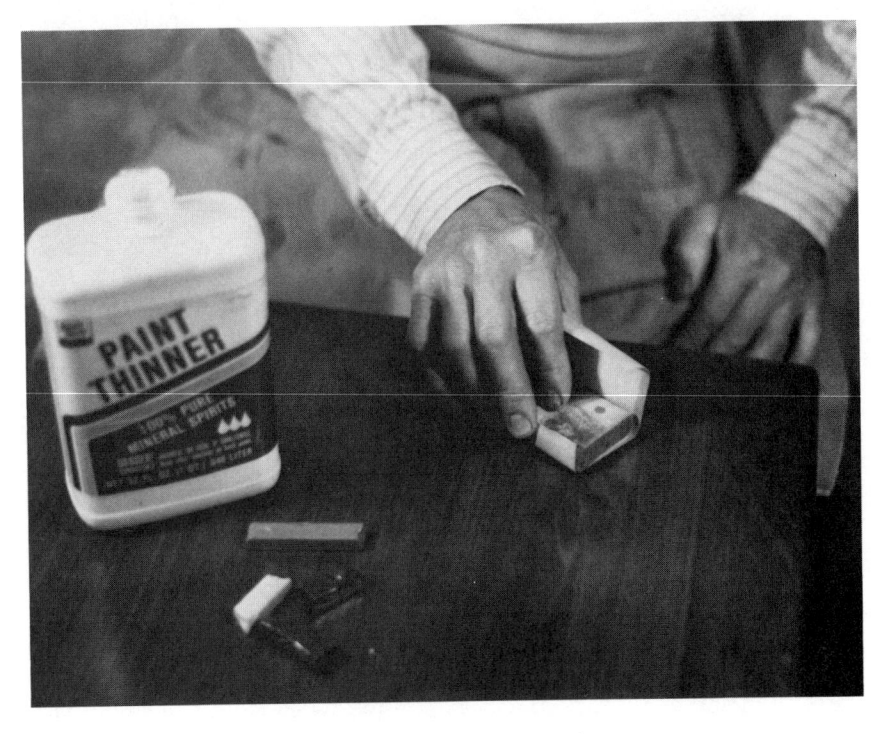

**15-3** When the hole is filled, sand the patched area smooth.

**15-4** Use steel wool to blend the sanded filler into the surrounding finish.

If the patch is rough or does not blend in with the finish, you can coat it with finish. Use a spray gun, an aerosol, or brush to apply the finish.

### Dents in unfinished wood

Steam out dents with water and a warm iron. Moisture causes the condensed wood to expand and swell out and level.

Wet the dent. On hardwood, poke small holes into the pores for moisture to enter. Place a wet cloth over the dent and heat the depression with a warm iron or soldering iron. When the dent rises, dry overnight and sand smooth.

### Scuff marks

Remove scuff marks on chair and table legs by rubbing with 3/0 or 4/0 fine steel wool that is wet with a cream or oil polish. See Chapter 13 to find out how to rub chair and table legs.

### Soft, sticky finishes

Soft and sticky finishes occur on chair arms, backs, and seats; around handles on cabinets; and on headboards of beds. This condition is caused by oil and perspiration from skin and hair, or humidity and pollution coming in contact with the finish over an extended period of time.

Rub the sticky surface with 4/0 fine steel wool wet with paint thinner. When clean, wax the surface. If the finish is soft all the way through, excessive rubbing with steel wool will remove all the finish and expose bare wood. If this happens, the finish must be removed and refinished.

## Warps in wood

A board warps because one side has more moisture than the other. The pores on the dry side shrink and pull together, bending the board. Warping often occurs on wood only finished on one side. The moisture on the finished side remains constant, while the moisture on the unfinished side dries out causing the board to bend.

To straighten a warp, wet the unfinished (concave) side. Place wet towels over the concave side, for a day or more, until the pores absorb moisture and swell and straighten. The board can then bend in the opposite direction. If this happens, wet the opposite side. If the opposite side is finished, remove the finish before wetting. When the board straightens and dries, finish the piece on both sides to prevent further warping.

## Worn edges

The edges of tops and furniture parts that have right angles are vulnerable to extra wear. Polishing, dusting, and rubbing wears the finish away, leaving a light or unfinished edge.

Mix stain or dry colors with lacquer. Apply by rubbing the color from the center of a flat brush 1/4 to 1 inch wide. Draw the brush along the bare edge with a light downward pressure, pulling finish from the center of the brush.

Touch-up pens filled with furniture colors can also be used to touch up bare edges.

## WATER DAMAGE

Cloudiness and hazing is often on, not in the finish. This type of damage can be removed by cleaning with a mild abrasive and oil.

White spots and rings in the finish caused by wet glasses and white spots from spilled water can be repaired. Rubbing the finish with oil and a mild abrasive will often remove the white blemish. The abrasive cuts off a thin layer of damaged finish, while the oil penetrates into the finish bringing it back to its original color.

Abrasives and oils that can be used include 4/0 steel wool dipped in oil, fine pumice stone and oil, or rottenstone and oil. Oils used with the abrasives could be: paraffin oil, boiled linseed oil, butter, mayonnaise, cream cleaning polish, mineral oil, or paste wax.

Lightly wiping the spot with camphorated oil might work. Quickly and gently whisking the surface with a lint-free cloth moistened with lacquer thinner might remove the spot. Be careful though; lacquer thinner will melt lacquer finishes. If the white spot disappears, wax the surface with a hard paste wax.

If none of these remedies are successful, sand the finish with 400-grit sandpaper and paint thinner. Then recoat with finish.

# Chapter 16

# Routine care of furniture

*M*ost furniture manufacturers provide instructions on how to care for their furniture. Often these directions are thrown away or lost. If followed, the instructions in this chapter should help your furniture look its best for many years of service and enjoyment.

## GLOSS FINISHES

Clean dirty gloss finishes with a damp cloth and thoroughly dry. Once or twice a year, apply a hard paste wax for gloss and protection. Always remove the old wax with paint thinner before rewaxing. In between waxing, about every three months, use a cream cleaning polish to clean the surface.

## SATIN OR SEMIGLOSS

Clean dirty surfaces with a damp cloth and thoroughly dry. Use a low-lustre cream cleaning polish every three months.

## OIL FINISHES

Occasionally coat oil and penetrating resin finishes with an oil polish. Wash dirty surfaces with paint thinner; dry and reoil. Wash damaged surfaces with paint thinner; then sand and recoat with the original finish product, linseed oil, tung oil, or commercially prepared penetrating resin finish.

## CANE FURNITURE

Unfinished cane acquires a dark patina over time. Do not mistake it for dirt. Dust both sides with a soft-bristle brush. Clean soil with a cloth dampened with a mild detergent, then thoroughly dry. Water, wet towels, or bathing suits that come in contact with cane will cause the finish to peel off.

## LEATHER CARE

Have you ever heard of waxing a cow or greasing a pig? I doubt it. Genuine furniture leather used on upholstery and tabletops is protected by a finish that needs no wax, polish, or oils.

Do not expose leather to sunlight. To remove dirt spots and spills, immediately wipe with a damp cloth and dry thoroughly. For heavily soiled surfaces, clean with a moist cloth soaked with Ivory flakes. When clean, dry and buff with a soft cloth. If after years of use the lather loses its luster, it can be waxed with a paste wax. Do not use saddle soap, cleaning solvents, liquid cleaning polish, oils, abrasive cleaners, detergents, or ammonia water on leather.

### Suede leather

Suede leather requires special cleaning methods. Save and follow the manufacturer's cleaning instructions.

### Leather repair

Leather furniture is finished much like wood furniture. An opaque color is applied over the leather, which is then grained and stippled. A protective finish is then added.

Scratches and small bare spots can be touched up with dry or oil colors mixed with lacquer or vinyl finish. On large touch-ups, spray clear vinyl finish or leather lacquer over the patch to protect it. Never spray wood lacquer over leather; it will crack when the leather bends. Only use lacquer that has been formulated for use on leather; it is called *leather lacquer*.

Brown, cordovan, and black shoe polish can be used to color light spots on leather when it will not be in contact with clothing.

## MARBLE CARE

Although marble is a hard and durable material, its polished surface is easily damaged. Marble should receive the same care as fine furniture. Use coasters under glasses and wipe up spilled liquids immediately. Protect marble from fruit juices, alcohol, tobacco, oil, carbonates, and acids because they will all etch the surface.

Periodically clean marble with warm water and a soft cloth. Once or twice a year wash with a mild detergent. A coat of colorless paste wax will give some protection, but never wax white marble because the wax might turn it yellow.

### Marble touch-up

Stains on marble can be erased by a gentle rubbing with a mixture of hydrogen peroxide and ammonia. Rinse the area in clear water and dry.

To remove dull spots and fine scratches, gently sand the dull area with 600-grit wet or dry sandpaper, using water as a lubricant. Then rub with putty powder (tin oxide), which is available in hardware stores. Sprinkle putty powder on the surface and rub with a soft wet cloth until the surface shines.

Major repairs should be made by a monument company. They have the grinding and polishing tools to make repairs.

## POLYESTER WET-LOOK FINISHES

Polyester wet-look finishes that are hardened with a catalyst are factory-applied finishes. They are characterized by their glasslike, high-gloss surface. Although these finishes are hard and durable, they are easily scratched and require professional repairing. Electric buffers and extra-fine rubbing compound is used to polish out scratches.

Dirt and food is easily removed with a soft, clean, damp cloth. Remove stubborn stains and smudges with a foamy nonammonia glass cleaner to lessen the chance of scratching or streaking the finish. Do not use furniture polishes because they tend to streak and leave a film that attracts dust.

Repairing dents and scratches in polyester requires professional help. The damaged area is sanded with 320-grit sandpaper to remove loose chips and assist in the binding of the patching material. Polyester patching compound and catalyst are mixed and applied to the hole; dried for 24 hours; then sanded smooth with 600-grit sandpaper. The final step is to buff to a high gloss with a buffer and extra-fine buffing compound.

## VINYL CARE

Vinyls require little care. An occasional cleaning with a damp cloth or mild detergent will keep it clean. There are many vinyl cleaners that work effectively without abrasive action.

### Vinyl repair

Holes, cuts, scratches, burns, and scuff spots in vinyl are repaired by using vinyl colors, vinyl patching compound, a heat gun or heat iron, and vinyl finishes. Professional vinyl repairing requires training and materials that are beyond the scope of this book.

Briefly, to repair a cut or hole in vinyl, a backing material is glued behind the cut vinyl. Liquid vinyl is applied to the hole and cured (hardened) with a heat gun similar to a hair dryer but much hotter. A matching vinyl grain pattern is pressed into the hardening vinyl with graining paper.

The hardened vinyl is either precolored or touched up with vinyl colors. A final coat of clear gloss or flat vinyl finish is sprayed over the patch. Vinyl finishes can be clear or opaque colors to match the color of the vinyl being repaired. If done properly, the repaired patch is undetectable.

Heavy vinyls are best repaired using a hot air gun. Vinyls that have cloth backings are best repaired using an electric heat iron. Here the hot iron is pressed over the liquid vinyl until it hardens. Thin vinyls, without backings, which would melt if heat were applied, are repaired with a cold, air-cured, vinyl patching compound.

## DO'S AND DON'TS FOR FURNITURE CARE

1. Immediately remove any liquids that are accidentally spilled on a finish, such as water, alcohol, cooking, or cleaning products. Blot with a soft cloth.
2. Use coasters or pads under drinks, flower pots, and other containers for liquids that are placed on tabletops.
3. Never leave a damp cloth on top of a finish. Water, solvents, or even furniture polish in the cloth could be trapped between the cloth and finish.
4. Do not expose furniture to high humidity. Excess moisture can cause wood to swell and split, finishes to loosen and peel. Avoid damp, cold areas such as porches, basements, and damp unheated rooms.
5. Furniture needs even temperatures. Extremes in temperatures can cause wood to expand and contract causing old or inelastic finishes to crack.
6. Do not expose furniture to direct sunlight. Stains in the wood under the finish will bleach, and the area exposed to the sun will be lightened. Sunlight shining through a glass window will eventually lighten a finish.
7. Use pads under hot dishes or pots on tabletops.
8. Do not leave a lit cigarette on a surface. It will quickly burn through the finish, charring it and the wood underneath.
9. Some rubber and soft plastic products stain and soften furniture finishes. Plastic grapes, doilies, coasters, and plastic tablecloths should be backed by cloth or felt unless they are labeled to be safe for use on furniture. Rubber bumpers attached to the bottom of old appliances, typewriters, and televisions might contain coal tar dye that can leave yellow stains in the finish.
10. Do not use polishes containing silicones. Many aerosol polishes contain silicones.
11. Use polishes recommended for furniture. Self-polishing floor waxes will soften furniture finishes.

12. When dusting or polishing, use a soft absorbent, lint-free cotton cloth, without buttons or seams. Rub with the grain of the wood.
13. Keep nail polish and nail polish remover away from tables. A spill will remove or damage the finish.

# Appendix
# Sources of finishing materials

The companies listed below sell finishing materials, wood, hardware, and tools. If the materials you need are not available locally, write one of these firms for a catalog. Most are free.

BINKS MANUFACTURING COMPANY
9201 West Belmont Ave.
Franklin Park, IL 60666
    Spray finishing equipment

CANE & BASKET SUPPLY COMPANY
1283 South Cochran Ave.
Los Angeles, CA 90019
    Cane, rush, reed, basketry, and caning books and tools

CONSTANTINE'S
2050 Eastchester Rd.
Bronx, NY 10461
    Hardwood, veneers, woodworking tools, furniture hardware, books, and wood finishes

CRAFTSMAN'S
1735 W. Cortland Ct.
Addison, IL 60101
    Hardwood, veneers, hand and power tools, upholstery supplies, and cabinet hardware

DEVILBIS COMPANY
Toledo, OH 43692
    Spray finishing equipment

HORTON BRASSES
P.O. Box 95, Nooks Hill Rd.
Cromwell, CN 06416
   Reproduction hardware (in both brass and hand-forged iron): drawer pulls, knobs, hinges, finials, and other hardware items

MOHAWK FINISHING PRODUCTS, INC.
Rt. 30 North
Amsterdam, NY 12010
   A complete line of furniture refinishing materials: finishes, stains, touch-up materials and tools, hardware, and vinyl repair supplies. A major supplier of finishing materials for factory and finishing shops.

STAR CHEMICAL CO., INC.
360 Shore Dr.
Hinsdale, IL 60521
   Finishing materials: finishes, stains, touch-up materials, hardware, and tools

TALAS
104 Fifth Ave.
New York, NY 10011
   Materials used to restore antiques; Renaissance wax.

WOOD FINISHING SUPPLY CO., INC.
1267 Mary Dr.
Macedon, NY 14502
   Finishing materials: shellac, tung oil, French polish, burn-in sticks, gold leaf, hide glue, paste wood filler, milk paint, and brass hardware. No minimum order required.

# Glossary

**abrasive**—A material used for wearing away a surface by friction; see *pumice stone, rottenstone, rubbing compound, sandpaper,* and *steel wool.*
**antique**—Furniture of a former period. Generally 100 years or older.
**alligatoring**—A varnish or lacquer finish that is cracked into large segments, resembling the hide of an alligator.
**aniline colors**—Colors made from coal tar products; also called water colors, spirit colors, and oil-soluble colors.
**antique finish**—Glazing color over a finish to give it the appearance of age.

**bleach**—A liquid chemical used to lighten the color of wood.
**bleeding**—Occurs when a stain or finish on the wood is dissolved by top coats and permeates into and discolors the top coat.
**blushing**—A white discoloration found on a lacquer surface while it is drying. Usually caused by spraying on cold rainy days when the humidity is high. To prevent or correct, add blush retarder to the finish before spraying.
**brushing lacquer**—A slow drying lacquer formulated for brushing.
**burning-in**—Filling dents in finishes by melting lacquer or shellac sticks into the dent.

**coat**—Finishing material applied to a surface.
**color-in-oil**—Pigmented colors mixed in linseed oil.

**dead flat**—Having no luster.
**denatured alcohol**—Grain alcohol poisonous for human consumption. Used to thin shellac.

**enamel**—Colored lacquer or varnish finishes that dry to a hard gloss or semigloss sheen.

**fish eyes**—Small, round cavities in a wet finish; usually caused by silicones in furniture polishes.
**flat lacquer**—Lacquer that dries with a dull rubbed effect.
**French polish**—An old method of applying a shellac finish. Applying several thin coats of shellac with a cloth.

**gilding**—Covering a surface with gold leaf or gold powder.
**glazing**—Applying a thin transparent coat of color with a cloth or brush over a painted or finished surface to produce a grain pattern or an antiqued appearance, or to soften the color.
**gloss**—The brightness of a smooth polished surface.
**grain**—The direction the wood's cell cavities run, either straight, curved, or on burl wood, irregular.

**hand rubbing**—Rubbing the final coat of finish by hand using an abrasive with a cloth or felt pad.

**in-the-wood finish**—A finish that soaks into the wood, hardening the inner fibers without a noticeable surface film; see *linseed oil, tung oil, penetrating resin sealer finish*.

**lacquer**—A fast-drying nitrocellulose finish that forms a hard film. Lacquers are sprayed.
**lifting**—The softening, wrinkling, and lifting of a dried finish by the solvents of another finish applied over it. Lacquer sprayed over varnish will often lift the varnish off the wood.
**linseed oil**—Oil pressed from seeds of the flax plant. An in-the-wood finish.

    *boiled linseed oil*—Dries throughout the coating, used on interior furniture and woodwork.

    *raw linseed oil*—Does not dry hard. For use on wood exposed to the elements.

**mineral spirits**—A solvent used to thin oil paint, varnish, and enamels; see *paint thinner*.

**oil colors**—Pastelike pigmented colors mixed in linseed oil.
**oil finish**—Finish that soaks into the wood, hardening the inner fibers; see *tung oil, linseed oil, penetrating resin finish*.
**on-the-wood finish**—A finish that produces a tough film on the surface of the wood; a finish that can be seen and touched; examples: lacquer, varnish, urethane, shellac, and paints.
**orange peel**—Bumps on the surface of a sprayed finish that resemble the skin of an orange. Caused by rapid drying. Add more thinner or use a slow-drying thinner.

**paint thinner**—A solvent used to thin oil paint, varnish, and enamels; also used to clean wax and oil off finishes. See *mineral spirits*.

**paste pore filler**—A thick paste used to fill the open pores of hard wood to obtain a smooth finish.

**patina**—The aging of finishes and wood produced by years of use and polishing.

**penetrating resin finish**—A commercially prepared in-the-wood finish that soaks into the wood, hardening the inner fibers without a noticeable surface film.

**pores**—Small holes or voids in hardwood that are the open ends of the tree's sap vessels. The direction they follow is called the grain pattern or grain of the wood. See *grain*.

**putty**—A thick, clear or colored paste used to fill dents and holes in wood. Can be thinned with linseed oil, lacquer thinner, or water.

**pumice stone**—A volcanic stone that is crushed to produce a fine abrasive. Used to rub finishes.

**remover**—A liquid that softens and removes old paint and finishes from wood. Also called paint remover.

**rottenstone**—A siliceous limestone used for high-gloss polishing.

**rubbing compound**—A rubbing abrasive in paste form. Used to rub finishes.

**sanding sealer**—A heavy-bodied lacquer or varnish finish used as a first coat to seal the wood. When sanded, it gives a smooth, level surface for top coats to be applied.

**satin**—A finish surface with a soft sheen similar to a satin material; see semigloss.

**sealer**—Any finish formulated to fill pores and stop penetration of top coats into the wood.

**semigloss**—A finish luster that is half way between gloss and flat.

**steel wool**—Fine threads of steel combined to form a pad; used to rub finishes.

**shellac**—The secretions of the lac bug, called lac, that is dissolved in alcohol and used as a finish. Shellac is an excellent sealer. It stops stains and sap from seeping into top coats.

**shellac stick**—Hard shellac in stick form colored to match finishes. Used to fill dents in finishes. See *burning in*. (The modern product is called *lacquer stick*).

**tack rag**—A tacky cheese cloth or lint-free cotton rag impregnated with varnish. Used to remove dust and dirt from surfaces prior to finishing.

**thinner**—A liquid used to thin finishing materials.

**touching up**—Repairing damaged finishes using fillers and colors, without resorting to refinishing.

**urethane**—(or *polyurethane*) A synthetic varnish finish that is tough and durable; excellent for kitchen and family room furniture.

**varnish**—A clear finish made with resins and oils. Made for brushing on furniture and woodwork.

**veneer**—A thin layer of wood glued over a less desirable surface to add beauty or strength.

**water white**—Any water-clear transparent finish.

# Bibliography

*Fine Woodworking*. Newton, Conn.: The Tauton Press, Inc.
　　A quarterly magazine devoted to furniture construction, and the proper use of wood-working tools and materials.

Grotz, George. 1962. *The Furniture Doctor*. Garden City, New York: Doubleday & Company.
　　Basic furniture refinishing.

Hoadley, Bruce. 1980. *Understanding Wood*. Newton, Conn.: The Tauton Press, Inc.
　　A comprehensive guide to wood and its properties.

Kinney, Parsons R. 1950. *The Complete Book of Furniture Repair and Refinishing*. New York, London: Charles Scribner & Sons.
　　Basic furniture refinishing.

McGiffin, Robert F. 1980. *Basic Furniture Care*. Peebles Island, Waterford, New York: New York State Office of Parks and Recreation, Division of Historic Sites Conservation and Collections Center.
　　Notes on antique care and conservation.

McGiffin, Robert F. 1989. *Furniture Care and Conservations*. Revised, 2nd ed. Nashville, Tenn.: AASLH Press, American Association for State and Local History.
　　Comprehensive step-by-step directions for examining, cleaning, repairing, and maintaining historical furniture.

Ormsby, Thomas H. 1951. *Field Guide to Early American Furniture*. New York: Bonanza Books.
　　Identifying antique furniture.

Scharff, Robert. 1956. *Complete Book of Wood Finishing*. New York, Toronto, London: McGraw-Hill Book Company, Inc.
    Basic furniture refinishing.

Yates, Raymond F. and Marguerite W. 1949. *A Guide to Victorian Antiques*. New York: Gramercy Publishing Co.
    Identifying antique furniture.

# Index

## A

abrasives (*see* sandpapers)
acrylic lacquer, 108
air compressors, 94
airless spray guns, 96
alcohol spots, 153
alcohol-soluble aniline stains, 60
aliphatic emulsion, 29
aliphatic glue, 30
alkyd resin varnish, 6
aluminum oxide sandpaper, 42, 43
ammonia for removing finishes, 20
aniline stains, 59-60
antique care/identification, 129-136
   authentication of antiques, 134-136
   cleaning, 130-134
   restoration process for antiques, 129-130
antiquing, 109-111
   stain used for, 67-72
   unfinished furniture, 127-128
automotive body putty, 39

## B

*Basic Furniture Care*, 134
belt sanders, 49
binder, finishes, 2
black spots, 57, 154
   bleaching, 57
bleaches, 20, 51-57
   black spot removal, 57
   Clorox laundry bleach (sodium hypochlorite) for, 52-53
   hydrogen peroxide, 54-56
   ink stain removal, 57
   miscellaneous compounds as, 57
   oxalic acid, 53-54
   preparation for, 51-52
   red stain removal with, 56-57
   selection guide to, 52-56
   trisodium phosphate, 56
bleeder spray guns, 95
blistered veneers, 33
Borden Cosco glue, 29
buffers, gloss finish using, 146
buildup wax, removal of, 150-152
burn-in sticks, filling dents and holes with, 40, 155-159
burned spots, 154

## C

candle wax on finish, removal, 154
cane furniture, care and cleaning, 161-162
caring for furniture, 161-165
China wood oil (*see* tung oil)
chlorinated lime bleaches, 57
clamping, 30-31
cleaning antiques, 130-134
Clorox laundry bleach (sodium hypochlorite), 52-53
closed coat sandpaper, 42, 43
compressors, 94
condensers, air compressor, 94
cracks, 33, 111
crayons, filling dents and holes with, 39
crazing, lacquer finish, 111
cream cleaning polishes, 151

## D

damaged wood (*see* repairs)
deluxing, 156
dents and holes, 36-40
   burn-in (shellac/lacquer) sticks for, 40, 155-159
   putty application to fill, 36-38
   putty on bare wood, 38-39
   putty on finished wood, 39-40
   sanding out, 46
dip tanks, removing finishes, 20-21
distressing, 109-111
dry sandpaper, 42, 44
Dutchman (*see* splits)

## E

edges, worn, 160
electric hand sanders, 48
Elmer's glue, 29
emery sandpaper, 42, 43
enamel paint, 8, 126
epoxy, 29
eye protection, xii-xiii

## F

filler and filling, 73-76
finishes, ix
   application, basic steps, 14-15, 77-93
   binder of, 2
   distressing, 109-111
   flat, 138, 140-141
   French polish, 87-89
   gilding, 92
   gloss, 139, 144-147, 161
   gold leaf, 92-93
   hand-rubbed, 137-147
   in-the-wood type, 9-12
   lacquer, 94-114, 126, 139
   linseed oil, 89
   milk paints, 85-86
   nontoxic, 12-14
   oil finishes, 139, 161
   on-the-surface type, 2-9, 2
   penetrating oil, 90-92
   pigment in, 2
   properties of, 2
   qualities to look for in, 2
   removal of (*see* removing finishes)
   rubbing, 137-139
   runs or drips, removal of, 85
   sanding prior to rubbing, 139-140
   satin, 138, 141-144, 161
   selection of, 1-15
   shellac, 86-87
   soft or sticky, 159-160
   spray gun selection vs. weight and consistency of, 96-97
   tack rag use for, 78-79

finishes, (cont.)
   testing to determine type, 21
   thinner or solvent in, 2
   tung oil, 90
   unfinished furniture, 115-128
   urethanes, 83-85, 126, 139
   varnish, 79-83, 125, 139
   vehicle of, 2
fire prevention, x
fish eyes, lacquer finish, 112
flat finish, 138
   beeswax or paraffin polish for, 151
   steel wool rubbing, 140-141
free cut sandpaper, 43
French polish finish, 87-89
fumes, ix
furniture selection, 1
furniture varnish, 5

## G

garnet sandpaper, 42, 43
gilding, 92
glazing, stain used for, 60, 67-69
gloss finish, 139, 144-147
   care of, 161
   electric buffer for, 146
   rottenstone rubbing, 144-145
gloves, xii
glue blocks, gluing, 34
gluing, ix, 27-35
   application techniques, 32
   clamping and, 30-31
   damaged wood repairs by, 33-35
   drying times, 31-32
   glue blocks for, 34
   glue selection guide, 27-30
   nails and staples, 35
   screws and, 35
   split edge repair, 34
   split wood repair, 33
   surface crack filling, 33
   veneer reattachment, 33
   wood plug regluing, 34
gold bronzing powder, gilding with, 92
gold leaf (see also gilding), 92-93

## H

hide glues, 29

highlighting, stain used for, 65
holes in wood (see dents and holes), 36
holes, lacquer finish, 112
hot spots, white spots, 154
hydrogen peroxide bleaches, 54-56
hydrosulphite bleaches, 57

## I

in-the-wood finishes, 9-12
   linseed oil, 9-10
   penetrating resin sealers, 11
   tung oil, 10-11
   wax finishes, 11
ink stains, bleaching, 57
interior varnish, 5

## L

lacquer, 8-9, 94-114, 126, 139
   air compressor and related equipment for, 94
   application techniques, 104-108
   bleaching with, 57
   coloring or staining with, 108
   cracking or crazing in, 111
   damage-resistance, 108
   distressing or antiquing, 109-111
   filling dents and holes with, 39
   fish eyes or holes, 112
   gloss, satin, flat finish, 108
   orange peel in, 137
   peeling off, 113
   pinholes in, 113
   removal of, 16
   runs, 113
   safety precautions with, 104
   sanding sealer, 104, 108
   sealer-type, application, 77
   shading with, 110-111
   spray booth for, 95
   spray guns (see spray guns), 95-99
   spraying technique for, 99-104
   streaks in, 113
   test to determine type, 21
   thinner for, 109
   turntable as work surface, 95
   types of, 108-109
   wet finish, will not dry, 114

   white marks in, 114
lacquer sticks, filling dents and holes with, 40
leather furniture, care and cleaning, 162
leather lacquer, 109, 162
lemon oil polish, 150
linseed oil finish, 9-10, 89
lye for removing finishes, 19, 21

## M

marble furniture, care and cleaning, 162-163
McGiffin, Robert F., 134
milk paint, 3
   application of, 85-86
   removal of, 26

## N

nail polish spots, removal of, 154
nails, regluing, 35
nitrocellulose, lacquer additive, 9
nonbleeder spray guns, 95
nontoxic finishes, 12-14
novelty lacquer, 109

## O

oil finishes, 139
   care of, 161
   linseed oil, 89
   penetrating oil, 90-92
   sealer-type, application, 78
   test to determine type, 21
   tung oil, 90
oil polishes, white, lemon, scratch-removing, 149-150
oil stains, 60-66
oil-soluble aniline stains, 60
oils, removal of, 16
oleoresinous varnish, 6
on-the-surface finishes, 2-9
   enamels, 8
   lacquer, 8-9
   milk paint, 3
   shellac, 3-5
   urethanes, 7
open coat sandpaper, 42, 43
orange peel, lacquer finishes, 137
orange shellac, 3
orbital sanders, 48
oxalic acid bleaches, 53-54

## P

paint
  enamel, 8, 126
  milk paint, 3, 26
  polishing surfaces, 152
  removal of, 16-20, 155
patina
  sanding antiques vs., 41-42
  staining antiques vs., 59
peeling lacquer finish, 113
penetrating oil finish, 90-92
penetrating resin sealers, 11, 78
phenolic-resin varnish, 6
picture-frame effect, stain used for, 65
pigmented oil stains, 60
pigments, 2
pinholes, lacquer finish, 113
plasticizer, lacquer additive, 9
polishing, 164-165, 148-152
  cream cleaning polishes, 151
  oil polishes, white, lemon, scratch-removing, 149-150
  painted surfaces, 152
  silicone polish buildup, removal, 152
  silicone polishes, 151-152
  waxing furniture, 148, 150-151
polyester wet-look finishes, care and cleaning, 163
polyurethane, 7
polyvinyl resin glue, 29
pore filling, 73-76
potassium permanganate bleaches, 57
powdered plastic resin glue, 29
pressure-feed spray guns, 95
pumice stone, satin finish using, 142-144
putties, filling dents and holes, 36-40

## R

red stains, removal with bleaches, 56-57
regulators, air compressor, 94
removing finishes, 16-26
  ammonia for, 20
  dip tanks for, 20-21
  lye for, 19, 21
  milk paint removal, 26
  remover application, 22-26
  safety precautions for, 21-22
  test for finish, 21
  trisodium phosphate for, 20
  wax-free removers for, 19
  wax-type removers, 17-19
repairs, 33-35, 153-160
  alcohol damage, 153
  black spots, 154
  burn spots, 154
  candle wax on finish, 154
  dents and holes, 36-40
  hot spots, white spots, 154
  nail polish stains, 154
  paint spots, 155
  scratches and dents, 155
  scuff marks, 159
  soft, sticky finish, 159-160
  warps in wood, 160
  water damage, 160
  worn edges, 160
resins, lacquer, 9
resorcinol resin glue, 30
restoration, antiques, 129-130
rosin/ester gum alkyd varnish, 6
rottenstone, gloss finish using, 144-145
rubbing varnish, 5
runs and drips
  lacquer finishes, 113
  removal of, 85

## S

sanding, 41-50
  antiques: patina and authenticity vs., 41-42
  belt sanders, 49
  blocks for, 47
  cleaning dirty sandpaper, 49-50
  electric hand sanders for, 48
  grit numbers, 43-45
  metal and finishes, sandpaper selection for, 43
  prior-to-rubbing, 139-140
  safety precautions for, 47
  sandpaper selection guide, 42-45
  scrapers, 49
  steel wool for, 50
  surface examination during, 46
  techniques for, 45-47
  tools and machines for, 47-50
  unfinished furniture, 122-124
  wood, sandpaper selection for, 43
sanding dust, putty made from, 39
sandpapers, 42-45
  abrasives used on, 42, 43
  block for, 47
  cleaning, 49-50
  grit numbers, 43-45
  metal and finishes, 43
  open vs. closed coat, 42, 43
  paper weight/strength rating, 42, 44
  wet/dry, 42, 44
  wood sanding, 43
sap ooze, sealing, 119
sap staining, 66
satin finish, 138, 141-144
  care of, 161
  pumice stone rubbing, 142-144
  steel wool rubbing, 141-142
scrapers, 49
scratch-removing oil, 150
scratches, 155
screws, regluing, 35
scuff marks, removal of, 159
sealers
  application of, 77-79
  lacquer over, 104, 108
  penetrating resin, 11
  penetrating-oil types, 91
  removal of, 16
  sap oozing and, 119
  stain and, 66
  unfinished furniture, 126
self-sealing stains, 66
semigloss finishes (see satin)
shellac, 3-5
  application techniques, 86-87
  "cut" number of, 86
  gloss finish, 87
  satin finish, 87
  sealer-type, application, 78
  test to determine type, 21
shellac sticks, filling dents and holes with, 40
silicone carbide sandpaper, 43
silicone polishes, 151-152
sodium hypochlorite bleaches (Clorox), 52-53, 57
sodium perborate bleaches, 57
soft finish, 159-160
solvents, 2, 9
spar varnish, 5
spirit varnish film, 6

splits
  edge (Dutchman), with grain, 34
glue repairs, 33
oblique edge, against grain, 34
spray booths, 95
spray guns
  adjustments, 97
  air hose position for, 97
  airless or hydraulic, 96
  bleeder vs. nonbleeder types, 95
  cleaning, 98-99
  clogs in, 113
  faulty finish patterns, troubleshooting guide for, 102-103
  handling, 97
  internal- vs. external-mix, 95
  parts of, 98
  pressure-feed type, 95
  selection of, finish material vs., 96-97
  technique for, 99-104
  vacuum-type, 95
staining, 58-72
  aniline stains for, 59-60
  antiquing, 67, 69-72
  application technique: oil stains, 62-66
  color selection, 67
  concentrated oil-base colors vs. premixed, 61
  drying time before final finish, 63
  glazing, 60, 67-69
  grains, opened and closed, application tips, 66-67
  highlighting with, 65
  lacquers for, 108, 110-111
  no-stain vs., 58
  oil stains, 60-66
  picture-frame effect with, 65
  red stain removal, bleaches for, 56-57
  scratch-removing oil, 150
  self-sealing types, 66
  unfinished furniture, 124-125
  uniforming color (sap staining), 66
  uses of, improving look of wood, 59
  varnish as, 66
  wood color and grain pattern vs., 66-67

staples, regluing, 35
steel wool, 50
  flat finish using, 140-141
  satin finish using, 141-142
sticky finish, 159-160
straight-line sanders, 48
streaks, lacquer finishes, 113
suede furniture, care and cleaning, 162
suppliers, 166-167
surfacing putty, 38

**T**

tack rags, 78
thinner, finishes, 2
thinner, lacquer, 109
Tite Bond glue, 29
tools, xi-xii
touch ups (*see* repairs)
trisodium phosphate, 20, 56
tung oil, 6, 10-11, 90
turntable, work surface, 95

**U**

unfinished furniture, 115-128
  antiquing, 127-128
  construction defects, correction of, 119-122
  enamel paint, 126
  finish application, 125-128
  finish selection, 118-119
  joint preparation: sanding, regluing, etc., 115-118
  lacquer finish, 126
  preparation of, 115-118
  sanding down, 122-124
  sealers for, 126
  sealing sap ooze, 119
  staining, 124-125
  urethane finish, 126
  varnish finish, 125
  wood preparation: filling, sanding, etc., 115-118
uniforming color of wood, 66
urethane resin varnish, 6
urethanes, 7, 126, 139
  application techniques, 83-85
  penetrating sealer and, 91
  sealer-type, application, 77
  test to determine type, 21

**V**

vacuum-type spray guns, 95
varathane, 7
varnish, 5-6, 139

application techniques, 79-83, 125
removal of, 16
sealer-type, application, 77
staining with, 66
test to determine type, 21
vehicle, finishes, 2
veneers
  blistered, 33
  loosened, regluing, 33
ventilation, ix-x
vinyl furniture, care and cleaning, 163-164

**W**

warped wood, 160
water putty, 39
water-soluble aniline stains, 60
wax finishes, 11
wax gilding, 92
wax putty sticks, filling dents and holes with, 40, 155-159
wax-free removers, removing finishes, 19
wax-type removers, removing finishes, 17-19
waxing furniture, 148, 150-151, 164-165
  buildup, removal of, 150-151
  flat finish, beeswax or paraffin, 151
  paste wax application, 150
  scratch-removing pastes, 151
waxy buildup, removal of, 150-152
Weldwood glue, 29
wet sandpaper, 42, 44
wet-look finishes, polyester, care and cleaning, 163
white glue, 29
white oil polish, 149
white shellac, 3
white spots, 114, 154
white zinc stearate sandpaper, 43
wood dough, 38
wood plugs, gluing, 34
woodworking tools, xi-xii
work surfaces, turntable for, 95
workbenches, x-xi
worn edges, 160

**Y**

yellow glue, 29